GOD COMFORTS ISRAEL

The Audience and Message of Isaiah 40-55

Debra Moody Bass

University Press of America,® Inc.
Lanham · Boulder · New York · Toronto · Oxford

Copyright © 2006 by
University Press of America,® Inc.
4501 Forbes Boulevard
Suite 200
Lanham, Maryland 20706
UPA Acquisitions Department (301) 459-3366

PO Box 317
Oxford
OX2 9RU, UK

All rights reserved
Printed in the United States of America
British Library Cataloging in Publication Information Available

Library of Congress Control Number: 2005936952
ISBN 0-7618-3347-1 (clothbound : alk. ppr.)
ISBN 0-7618-3348-X (paperback : alk. ppr.)

∞™ The paper used in this publication meets the minimum
requirements of American National Standard for Information
Sciences—Permanence of Paper for Printed Library Materials,
ANSI Z39.48—1984

CONTENTS

Introduction	v
Chapter 1. The Situation of the People of Israel in Judah and Babylonia during the Exilic Period	1
Chapter 2. The Audience(s) of Deutero-Isaiah The Scholars' Opinions	31
Chapter 3. The Agenda of Comfort in Deutero-Isaiah	91
Chapter 4. Conclusion	127
Bibliography	133
Index	141

INTRODUCTION

GOD COMFORTS ISRAEL: THE AUDIENCE AND THE MESSAGE OF ISAIAH 40-55

Chapters 40-55 of the book of Isaiah, also known as Second Isaiah or Deutero-Isaiah, begin with the command, "Comfort ye, comfort ye, my people," and conclude with an address to herald Zion/Jerusalem to announce God's coming. A focus of many scholars in the past has been to determine what the comfort entails. But the question remains as to who is to be comforted and who is to do the comforting. This question highlights the importance of identifying the audiences in Deutero-Isaiah.

This dissertation will deal with two basic problems regarding the audience in Deutero-Isaiah. The first problem concerns the lack of clarity regarding the intended audiences. Just who are Deutero-Isaiah's audiences and how do they relate to the groups that are mentioned in the text? The problem of the lack of clarity concerning the audiences relates to Deutero-Isaiah's explicit references to several groups. For the purposes of this study they are categorized in four groups: (1) the people in exile, (2) Jacob/Israel, (3) Zion/Jerusalem, and (4) Babylon-Cyrus, together with the Nations.

The second problem with respect to the audiences is the common neglect of the full character of God's comfort, which will be seen to include the land and "the ends of the earth." For Deutero-Isaiah, God's comfort is not complete without the return to Jerusalem and the offer of salvation to the nations. Scholars often fail to appreciate the full range of comfort as including both the assurance to the people in exile and preparing the land for the people's return, the proper place from which they can carry out their task of being God's servant. In this light, Deutero-Isaiah's message of comfort becomes a key to identifying the complete range of audiences and in understanding details of his agenda of comfort.

The methodology will involve an investigation of the full nature of God's plan of comfort in the book of Deutero-Isaiah. It includes an attempt to address the issues of the audience through a study of the motif of comfort. I will examine the several audiences that are the recipients of this comfort as well as re-examine the traditional models and arguments for the plan of comfort. I will discuss how the realization of the comfort involves transformation for the people in exile, those left in Judah, the Diaspora, and the nations.

This dissertation will be organized in four chapters. The first chapter will revisit the historical setting presented by the biblical accounts and other sources, including archaeological information. This chapter will focus on four areas: 1) Judah under attack; 2) the people remaining in Judah after the deportations; 3) the Exiles in Babylonia; and 4) the Egyptian Gola. Chapter two presents the positions of seven commentators and four scholars who focus on the social and political perspective. In this chapter I will give an analysis of the audiences explicitly addressed in Deutero-Isaiah by revealing how the ambiguity of the texts have created problems in regards to identity and location.

Chapter three analyzes the texts that use the word *nhm* as a strategy to determine the agenda of comfort for Deutero-Isaiah and again brings some clarity as to who the audiences are. The role "Servant Israel" is to play in God's plan of comfort becomes more evident in this chapter and more inclusive in nature and focus. For one of the tasks assigned to the Servant is to proclaim the salvation of God to "the ends of the earth."

Chapter four, the final chapter, summarizes the results and significance of the study.

CHAPTER 1

THE SITUATION OF THE PEOPLE OF ISRAEL IN JUDAH AND BABYLONIA DURING THE EXILIC PERIOD

JUDAH UNDER ATTACK
Textual Evidence

The Events of 598/97 B.C.E.

In 2 Kgs 24-25, we find a vivid account of selected events that took place in 598/97 B.C.E.[1] Jehoiakim was the King of Judah for eleven years and for the latter of those years he served as a real or putative vassal under Nebuchadrezzar, King of Babylon. Yet, he turned and rebelled against Nebuchadrezzar. As punishment, Nebuchadrezzar sent some of his forces against Judah, including some Arameans, Moabites, and Ammonites. As the Babylonian army approached, Jehoikim died, under unknown circumstances, and his son, Jehoiachin, who was only eighteen at the time, began to rule as king. Before Jehoiachin completed three months as king, Babylon came up against Judah and this time we are told in 2 Kgs 24:11-14:[2]

King Nebuchadnezzar of Babylon advanced against the city while his troops were besieging it. Thereupon King Jehoiachin of Judah, along with

---

[1] Throughout this study, the three deportation dates noted are: 598/97, 587/86, 582 B.C.E.

[2] The translation used throughout this work is the NJPS.

his mother, his courtiers, commanders, and officers, surrendered to the king of Babylon. The king of Babylon took him captive in the eighth year of Nebuchdrezzer's reign. He carried off from Jerusalem all the treasures of the House of the Lord and the treasures of the royal palace; he stripped off all the golden decorations in the Temple of the Lord - which King Solomon of Israel had made - as the Lord had warned. He exiled all of Jerusalem: all the commanders and all the warriors – ten thousand exiles - as well as all the craftsmen and smiths; only the poorest people in the land were left.

After this first deportation, amounting to 10,000 men (presumably plus their families), and an unstated number of craftsmen (with their families), Nebuchadrezzar placed Jehoiakim's brother Mattaniah, another son of Josiah, as king over Israel and changed his name to Zedekiah (2 Kgs 24:17).

The Events of 587/86 B.C.E.

Zedekiah, like those before him, soon brought forth the wrath of Nebuchadrezzar. He became even more involved with Egypt (Jeremiah 37-38) and enlisted its support in a rebellion against Nebuchdrezzar. In retaliation, the Babylonian army attacked Jerusalem, beginning in the ninth year, the tenth month, tenth day, of Zedekiah's reign. The city was besieged until famine prevailed on the eleventh year, fourth month, ninth day - thus a siege of eighteen months (2 Kgs 25:3). Zedekiah and all the men of war fled by night, the king fleeing toward Transjordan. He and his sons were captured in the plains of Jericho. From there they were taken to the Babylonian headquarters in Riblah, in Syria, where King Zedekiah witnessed the slaying of his sons just before his own eyes were put out. Zedekiah was then put in chains of brass and carried off to Babylonian captivity (2 Kgs 25:7). This initiated the second deportation. This second time was the most devastating for Jerusalem, according to the text:

On the seventh day of the fifth month - that was the nineteenth year of King Nebuchadrezzar of Babylon - Nebuzaradan, the chief of the guards, an officer of the king of Babylon, came to Jerusalem. He burned the House of the Lord, the king's palace, and all the houses of Jerusalem; he burned down the house of every notable person. The entire Chaldean force that was with the chief of the guard tore down the walls of Jerusalem on every side. The remnant of the people that was left in the city, the defectors who had gone over to the king of Babylon - and the remnant of the population - were taken into exile by Nebuzaradan, the chief of the guards. But some of the poorest in the land were left by the chief of the guards, to be vinedressers and field hands. 2 Kgs 25:8-12

By the end of 587/86 B.C.E., according to 2 Kgs 25, there was great devastation of the land, the houses, and the walls. The Temple treasures became booty and an unnumbered amount of people were taken off into captivity by the Babylonians.

The Events after 587/86 B.C.E.

Gedaliah, son of Ahikam son of Shaphan, became Babylon's chosen local representative and tried to persuade the people to live under the Babylonian rule. Gedaliah set up headquarters in Mizpah, north of Jerusalem. Some of the remnant of Judah's army went to meet with him there. These men were Ishmael, son of Nethaniah, Johanan the son of Careah, Seraiah the son of Tanhumeth the Netophathite, and Jaazaniah the son of a Maachathite, and their men (2Kgs 25:23; Jer 40:7-10). Gedaliah affirmed that they had nothing to fear under the rule of the Babylonians as long as they served the king of Babylon (2 Kgs 25:24). Yet, shortly thereafter, Ishmael son of Nethaniah son of Elishama, who was of royal descent and may have been a pretender to the "throne"(2 Kgs 25:25), returned to Mizpah with a small force and assassinated Gedaliah and all those in Mizpah serving in his administration (2 Kgs 25:25; Jeremiah 52). Many of the remaining people of Judah responded to this chaos by fleeing to Egypt: And all the people, young and old, and the officers of the troops set out and went to Egypt because they were afraid of the Chaldeans. 2 Kgs 25:26

Chapters 24 and 25 of 2 Kings have provided much information about what went on just prior to the attacks by Nebuchadrezzar and after the three deportations. However, the numbers of persons deported vary according to the biblical accounts. The two major sources of data are Jeremiah 29, 39, and 52 and 2 Kings 24-25 (2 Chron. 36 records no numbers).

1st Deportation

II CHRON 36:5-21	II KINGS 24-25	JEREMIAH 29;39;52
Jehoiakim was twenty-five years old when he became king, and he reigned eleven years in Jerusalem. King Nebuchadrezzar of Babylon marched against him; he bound him with fetters to convey him to Babylon. Nebuchadrezzar also brought some vessels of the House of the Lord to Babylon, and set them in his palace in Babylon...Jehoichin... reigned three months and	All Jerusalem: the King, his mother, his courtiers, all the commanders and officers, and all the warriors - 10,000 exiles - as well as craftsmen and smiths. (24:14) 7,000 -- all warriors and 1,000 craftsmen/smiths (24:16) 8th year of Nebuchdrezzar (24:12) Jehoichin was king at 18 years of age	The priests, prophets, the rest of the elders of the exile community ...after King Jeconiah, the queen mother, the eunuchs, the officials of Judah and Jerusalem, and the craftsmen and smiths... (29:1-3) 3,023 (52:28) exiles 7th year of Nebuchadrezzar (52:28) 3,023 exiles

4 God Comforts Israel

ten days in Jerusalem.... reigned only three months
At the turn of the year, King Nebuchadrezzar sent to have him brought to Babylon with the precious vessels of the House of the Lord, and he made his kinsman Zedekiah king over Judah and Jerusalem.

2nd Deportation

II CHRON 36:5-21	II KINGS 24-25	JEREMIAH 29;39;52
He (God) therefore brought the king of the Chaldeans upon them, who killed their youths by the sword in their sanctuary; He did not spare youth, maiden, elder, or graybeard, but delivered all into his hands. All the vessels of the House of the Lord and the treasures of the king and his officers were all brought to Babylon. They burned down all its mansions, and consigned all its precious objects to destruction. Those who survived the sword he exiled to Babylon, and they became his son's servants till the rise of the Persian kingdom, in fulfillment of the word of the Lord spoken by Jeremiah, until the land paid back its sabbaths; as long as it lay desolate it kept sabbath, till seventy years were completed.	The remnant left, the defectors who had gone over to the king of Babylon and the remnant of the population, but some of the poorest in the land were left to be vinedressers and field hands. (25:11-12) 19th year of Nebuchadrezzar (25:8) 9th year, 10th month, 10th day of Zedekiah (25:1) All the people, young and old, and the officers of the troops set out to Egypt because they were afraid of the Chaldeans (25:26) 7th month, 19th year Nebuchadrezzar	Exiles from Jerusalem (52:29); The Chaldeans burned down the king's palace and the house of the people by fire and they tore down the walls of Jerusalem. The remnant...and the defectors... were exiled. But some of the poorest people who owned nothing were left in the land...he gave them vineyards and fields at that time (39:9-10) 19th year of Nebuchadrezzar 10th day, 5th month (52:12-13); 11th year, 9th day, 4th month of Zedekiah (39)

3rd Deportation

II CHRON	II KINGS	JEREMIAH 52:30
		745 Judeans exiled in the 23rd year of Nebuchdrezzar (52:30). In all, 4600 were taken away.

These are numbers from the texts that have been preserved. The numbers differ (2 Kgs 25=18,000+; Jer 41:16-18=4600) and their interpretations vary among scholars.

Apparently many Judeans regarded Jehoiachin as the true king, even if he was in exile, as suggested also by Jer 28:4. Whatever the case, the conclusion of 2 Kgs 25 ends with a happy note. The successor new king of Babylon, King Evil-merodach, has released King Jehoichin from prison in his 37th year (561 B.C.E.). His prison garments were removed and he was invited to sit at the King's table. He received a regular allotment of food each day he remained in Babylon (2 Kgs 25:27-30; Jer 52:31-34).

Chronicles of Chaldean Kings and Josephus

A major extra-biblical resource recording the military activity of Babylon is known as the Chronicles of Chaldean Kings. These cuneiform texts cover the Kassite Period (16th-14th centuries B.C.E.) to the Seleucid era (198-140 B.C.E.).[3] Wiseman covers the period of 626 B.C.E. to 556 B.C.E. This time period records the first conquest of Hatti (Judah) in 605 B.C.E. (battle at Carchemish), the first deportation from Jerusalem (598/97), and several battles that ensued due to rebellion (596, 595, 594, 557 B.C.E.).

Events of 598/97 B.C.E..

The Chronicles of Chaldean Kings gives a brief account of the operations that took place in 598/97 B.C.E. It records that Nebuchadrezzar "besieged Jerusalem" and "seized it on the second day of the month of Adar. He then captured its king and appointed a king of his own choice." Nebuchadrezzar "received heavy tribute from the city, which he sent back to Babylon."[4] The Chronicle does not go into detail about the siege and how it came about, but it does record the results according to Wiseman.

---

[3] Donald John Wiseman, Chronicles of Chaldean Kings (London: The Trustees of the British Museum, 1956), 1.

[4] Wiseman, 33.

Although no details of siege are given, the Chronicle clearly expresses the result. The king of Jerusalem was captured, a substitute chosen by Nebuchadrezzar was placed on the throne and considerable tribute collected and sent back to Babylon. Jehoiachin's place was taken by a Babylonian nominee, the young uncle of Jehoichin named Mattaniah whose official name was designated or changed to Zedekiah.[5]

According to Josephus, Jehoiachim refused to pay tribute to Babylon in 598/97 B.C.E. perhaps following the lead of the Egyptians. But rather than Egypt being targeted, it was Syria-Palestine, which included Judah, that bore the wrath of Nebuchadrezzar's military army.

> On the third year, upon hearing that the king of the Babylonians made an expedition against the Egyptians, he did not pay tribute, yet was he disappointed of his hope, for the Egyptians durst not fight at this time. And indeed the prophet Jeremiah foretold every day, how vainly they relied on their hopes from Egypt, and how the city would be overthrown by the king of Babylon, and Jehoikim the king would be subdued by him.[6]

Wiseman quotes Josephus' account of the events of 598/97 B.C.E. although it differs somewhat from his summary of the events.

> Now a little time after [the revolt of Jehoikim], the king of Babylon made an expedition against Jehoiakim, whom he received [into the city], and this out of fear of the foregoing predictions of this prophet, as supposing that he should suffer nothing that was terrible, because he neither shut the gates, nor fought against him; yet when the Babylonian was come into the city, he did not observe the covenant he had made, but he slew such as were in the flower of their age, and such as were of the greatest dignity, together with their king Jehoiakim, whom he commanded to be thrown before the walls, without any burial; and made his son Jehoiachin king of the country, and of the city: he also took of the principal persons in dignity for captives, three thousand in number, and led them away to Babylon; among which was the prophet Ezekiel, who was then but young. And this was the end of king Jehoiakim,... But a terror seized on the king of Babylon, who had given the kingdom Jehoiachin, and that immediately: he was afraid that he should bear him a grudge, because of his killing his father, and thereupon should make the country revolt from him; wherefore he sent an army, and besieged Jehoiachin in Jerusalem; but because he was of a gentle and just disposition, he did not desire to see the city endangered on his account, but he took his mother, and kindred, and delivered them to the commanders sent by the

---

[5] Wiseman, 33.

[6] Flavis Josephus, <u>Antiquities X. 6</u>, quoted by Donald J. Wiseman. <u>Chronicles of Chaldean Kings,</u> 33.

king of Babylon, and accepted of their oaths, that neither should they suffer any harm, nor the city; which agreement they did not observe for a single year, for the king of Babylon did not keep it, but gave orders to his generals to take all that were in the city captives both the youth and the craftsmen, and bring them bound to him; their number was ten thousand eight hundred and thirty-two; as also Jehoiachin and his mother and friends. And when these were brought to him, he kept them in custody, and appointed Jehoiachin's uncle Zedekiah to be king;...[7]

According to Wiseman, this account suggests that Nebuchadrezzar returned to Jerusalem early in his seventh year and killed Jehoiakim.[8] He acknowledges that Josephus finds some support in II Chronicles 36:6.

> Jehoiakim was twenty-five years old when he became king, and he reigned eleven years in Jerusalem; he did what was displeasing to his God. King Nebuchadrezzar of Babylon marched against him; he bound him in fetters to convey him to Babylon.

The Chronicles of Chaldeans Kings does not mention Nebuchadrezzar after his 11th year of reign (594/3 B.C.E.). The tablets resume in the year 557/6 B.C.E. with Neriglissar as king.

Archaeological Evidence

The 6th century B.C.E. has been illuminated by recent archaeology. The destruction levels at many of the sites uncovered give evidence of Babylonian invasions and conquests.[9] Many sites in Philistia and in Judah have revealed the extent of the destruction. This new evidence testifies to the vast destruction brought about by the Babylonian military campaigns.

---

[7] Josephus, 35.

[8] Josephus, 35.

[9] Amihai Mazar, "The Babylonian Period", <u>Archaeology of the Land of the Bible</u>. (New York: Doubleday, 1990), 548.

The archaeological finds at Lachish (Tell ed-Duweir) fit with the upheavals and crises that are mentioned in the Book of Jeremiah (34:7). These finds support the biblical reports of the Babylonian campaigns of 598/7 and 587/86 B.C.E.

As for Jerusalem, archaeological work has revealed the remains of homes on the eastern slopes of the Ophel that were destroyed by fire. In addition, many sherds and other artifacts discovered on that hill and around the Temple area have been dated to the last years of the Judean monarchy.[10] Yet the search for archaeological traces in Jerusalem in Iron Age III has had minimal success for several reasons:

> The dense cover of modern construction, the presence of holy places and the ideological-religious bias accompanying a considerable proportion of the hypotheses and interpretations of excavations have discouraged many archaeologists, who have therefore limited themselves to studies of the topography of the city in light of the biblical evidence.[11]

K. Kenyon and Y. Shiloh have excavated the area known as the City of David. Their work has uncovered the architecture of some houses in the Iron Age III. These houses were apparently built in the seventh century B.C.E. but evidence shows they were probably destroyed in 586 B.C.E. during the Babylonian raid.[12] Discoveries on the Western Hill have revealed the presence of a large tower, approximately eight meters in height. Evidence suggests that the "tower was abutted by a floor showing traces of fire and destruction, along with sherds of the Iron Age III and four arrowheads, evidence of the battle that raged here in 586 B.C.E."[13]

Excavations at various Judean sites prove that some towns suffered total destruction at this time. This includes the cities of Lachish (Tell ed-Duweir), Tell Beit Mirsim, Kadesh Barnea (Tell el-Qudeirat), and Tel Batash.[14] Kenyon says the following in regards to excavations in Jerusalem.

---

[10] Gaalyah Cornfeld and Noel Freedman, Archaeology of the Bible, Book by Book. (San Francisco: Harper and Row, 1976), 177.

[11] G. Barkay, "Iron Age II-III", The Archaeology of Ancient Israel (New Haven: The Open University of Israel, 1992), 364-65.

[12] Barkay, 368.

[13] Barkay, 368.

[14] Barkay, 373.

The excavation evidence from many sites, for instance Tell Beit Mirsim, Beth Shemesh, and Tell Duweir, is that town and village life was severely disrupted...Jerusalem was therefore left in ruins, inhabited by some of the poorest of the land, left to be vinedressers and ploughmen.[15]

The chronicles of the Chaldean kings, cuneiform texts of the history of Babylonia, are also a reliable source of knowledge. Only a few of the texts have survived, but they seem to have recorded the principal national events of Babylon from the Kassite period (16-14 centuries B.C.E.) to the end of the Seleucid era (198-149 B.C.E.).[16] Chronicle tablet B.M. 21946 records the events beginning with the twenty-first year of Nabopolassar (605/4 B.C.E.) through the eleventh year of the reign of Nebuchadrezzar (594/3 B.C.E.). It is in this tablet that we find a brief mention of the capture of Jerusalem and the first deportation in 598/7 B.C.E.:

In the seventh year, the month of Kislev (Dec), the King of Akkad mustered his troops, marched to the Hatti-land, and encamped against the city of Judah and on the second day of the month of Adar he seized the city and captured the king. He appointed there a king of his own choice, received its heavy tribute and sent (them) to Babylon.[17]

Wiseman identifies "Hatti-land" as Syria-Palestine.[18] Unfortunately there is no Babylonian record to complement the biblical account of the total destruction which occurred in 587/86 B.C.E.

---

[15] Kathleen M. Kenyon, Digging Up Jerusalem. (N.Y.:Praeger Publishers, 1974), 172.

[16] Wiseman, 1.

[17] Wiseman, 73.

[18] Wiseman, 33.

Ephraim Stern states that the Babylonian Chronicle is a main source of information, but because it ends in 594 B.C.E., it stops short of providing the necessary information needed to fill in the gaps between 594 B.C.E. and the Persian conquest in 538 B.C.E.[19] He tries to explain why there is so little evidence in support of the Babylonian presence in Judah:

> Although the Babylonians created a new administrative organization, different from that of their predecessors, this did not leave any clear traces in the country's archaeological record....During the Babylonian period, the main foreign influence in Palestine remained Mesopotamian culture. In many cases, this makes it almost impossible to determine if a certain artifact with Babylonian parallels should be dated to the late Assyrian period, to the Babylonian period, or even to the early Persian period. During all three periods, Palestine absorbed influences from the same remote Mesopotamian center.[20]

However for Stern, this ambuiquity does not deny the extent of the devastation that the Babylonian military campaigns inflicted on Palestine and its surrounding areas.

Subsequently, the most prominent feature left by 70 years of Babylonian domination in Palestine was the total destruction and devastation of all the main cities that had flourished during the Assyrian period, even those fortresses established by the Assyrian authorities themselves.[21]

Stern forms this opinion based on the results of archaeological excavations conducted throughout Palestine.

> A survey of results of all the archaeological excavations conducted in Palestine (minus regions of Phoenicia, Benjamin, and Transjordan) reveals that all its cities lay in ruins by the end of the Babylonian period.... Archaeological findings for the Babylonian period throughout Palestine include massive destruction levels, a few weapons..., and some seals and seal impressions....[22]

---

[19] Ephraim Stern, "The Babylonian Period", Archaeology of the Land of the Bible, (NewYork: Doubleday, 2001), Part 2, 303.

[20] Stern, 308.

[21] Stern, 308-309.

[22] Stern, 309.

Finally, Stern concludes the following:

> The bottom line in this discussion is that after the Babylonian conquest of Judah, only in the small region of Benjamin did some sites continue to exist or were rebuilt, while the rest of the country remained in a state of total destruction and near abandonment.[23]

The People Left in Palestine after the Deportations

Textual Evidence

Reports of the deportations recorded in the 2 Chr 33:20-21; 2 Kgs 24-25 and Jeremiah 29, 39 and 52, initially give the impression that all the people were taken off into captivity:

> Those who survived the sword he exiled to Babylon, and they became his and his sons' servants till the rise of the Persian kingdom, in fulfillment of the word of the Lord spoken by Jeremiah, until the land paid back its sabbaths; as long as it lay desolate it kept sabbath, till seventy years were completed. - 2 Chr 36:20-21

In other passages this perspective is modified and we learn that the poor in the land (*dlt ers*) were left to be vinedressers and field hands (2 Kgs 25:12; Jer 40:7; 52:16). Then in Jer 40:11-12, we read that some migrated to the land of Benjamin, north of Jerusalem, if only for a brief period during the time of Gedaliah which lasted about 3 months:

> Likewise, all the Judeans who were in Moab, Ammon, and Edom, or who were in their lands, heard that the king of Babylon had let a remnant stay in Judah, and that he had put Gedaliah son of Ahikam son of Shaphan in charge of them. All these Judeans returned from all the places to which they had scattered. They came to the land of Judah, to Gedaliah at Mizpah, and they gathered large quantities of wine and figs. Jer 40:11-12.

In this text, it is clearly stated that, at least briefly, there were people living in the north other than the "poorest in the land" after the second deportation of 587/86. Some of the remaining social classes who had been able to escape into other areas, appear to have returned to the area once they heard that things in Benjamin, i.e., northern Judah were settling down, to participate in the harvesting of the crops. However, after the assassination of Gedaliah, this "remnant" concluded that they needed to leave Mizpah and flee to Egypt:

---

[23] Stern, 326.

> And they went and stayed at Geruth Chimham near Bethlehem, intending to go to Egypt because of the Chaldeans; for they were afraid of them, because Ishmael...had slain Gedaliah...whom the King of Babylon had made governor over the land. Jer 41:17

Again we are given the impression from the biblical evidence that although there were a few areas in the realm of Judah spared total devastation by the Babylonians, Jerusalem was abandoned due to the political turmoil of the day. W. F. Albright, the leading Palestinian archaeologist of his day, said the following over forty years ago:

> A fair number of towns and fortresses of Judah have now been excavated in whole or in part; many other sites have been carefully examined to determine the approximate date of their last destruction. The results are uniform and conclusive: many towns were destroyed at the beginning of the 6th century B.C.E. and never again occupied; others were destroyed at that time and partly reoccupied at some later date; still others were destroyed and reoccupied after a long period of abandonment, marked by a sharp change of stratum and by intervening indications of use for non-urban purposes. There is not a single case known where a town of Judah proper was continuously occupied through the Exilic period. [24]

Albright's opinion was a reflection of the scholarly consensus of his day. This perspective is affirmed most recently by E. Stern, while noting that northern Judah, i.e. Benjamin, was another story.[25]

Social and Political Conditions

The plight of those remaining in Judah after the first two deportations (592 and 587/86 B.C.E.) was a difficult one according to Lam 1:11; 2:12, 20; 4:4,10. Extreme famine, leading to cannibalism, was widespread. Neighboring peoples took advantage of the situation and took over land previously belonging to Judah (Jer 32:44; 49:1; Ezek 26:2; 25:25; 35:10). Jerusalem was vulnerable because of the destruction of the walls effected by the Babylonian armies. Those remaining in the land were exposed to all kinds of invasions, even politically, geographically, and religiously. In accord with the archaeological picture of the Babylonian period, the book of Lamentations creates a dark and dim picture of the situation after the attack of 587/86 B.C.E. and the second deportation:

---

[24] W.F. Albright, Archaeology of Palestine (London:Pelican, 1956), 141.

[25] Stern, 326.

All her inhabitants sigh as they search for bread;
They have bartered their treasures for food, to keep themselves alive. Lam 1:11

Her gates have sunk into the ground,
He has smashed her bars to bits. Lam 2:9

Our heritage is passed to aliens,
Our homes to strangers.
We must pay to drink our own water,
Obtain our own kindling at a price. Lam 5:2, 4

After the conquest, Judah presumably comprised the territory extending from just north of Bethel to south of Beth-zur and from the Jordan River to just west of Emmaus and Azekah. This would be an area of about twenty-five miles north to south and thirty or so miles east to west - about 800 square miles, to judge from the books of Ezra and Nehemiah.[26] A recent completed study of the survey of Judah "divides Judaea into two major sections, North, extending from the southern border of Benjamin to just north of Hebron; and South, incorporating the area from Hebron to the Negev sits."[27] After the exile of Zedekiah, the Babylonians selected Mizpah of Benjamin as the administrative center for the region under the leadership of Gedaliah son of Ahikam son of Shaphan (2 Kgs 25:23). Mizpah was chosen presumably because it was not destroyed by Babylonian forces and was centrally located. It continued as the Babylonian/Persian administration center for over a century.[28] Gedaliah's position is documented in 2 Kgs 25:24-25 and Jer 40:10; 41:3. Here it appears that there were some Chaldean soldiers and other servants left by Nebuzaradan, captain of the Babylonian troops, to guard and perhaps oversee the loyalty of Gedaliah. Gedaliah set up a local administration.[29] However, this was obviously not enough protection. Under the influence and prompting of the Ammonite king, the Judean Ishmael, of the royal seed, and a small group of followers assassinated Gedaliah, all his administration and the Chaldeans who were assigned to Mizpah (2 Kgs. 25:25-26). According to the 2 Kgs 25:26, those

---

[26] J. Maxwell Miller and John H. Hayes, A History of Ancient Israel and Judah. (Phila: Westminster, 1986), 446.

[27] Charles E. Carter, The Emergence of Yehud in the Persian Period: a social and demographic study (Sheffield: Sheffield Academic, 1999), 54.

[28] Miller and Hayes, 424.

[29] Miller and Hayes, 421.

remaining in the area then fled for their own safety, fearing retaliation from Nebuchadrezzar.

The biblical accounts found in 2 Kings 25 and Jeremiah 52 state that the "poor in the land" were left to be vinedressers and field hands. Doubtless, this group was not part of the administration in Mizpah. But the text does not reveal any particular details about who "the poorest in the land" were. Some people must have continued in the area, even though the archaeological evidence as summarized by Stern, does not show traces of these people. Since the "poor in the land" were not considered worthy of being counted, the number of people left in the land can not be estimated, as mentioned, and archaeological traces of their presence outside Benjamin eluded the archaeologists.

The territory of Benjamin offers a different picture. In his comments about Jerusalem, Berquist mistakenly equates the situation of Benjamin with that of Jerusalem. So he states the following about the situation:

> The social structure continued to include some hierarchicalization. Village elders remained and were probably as influential as ever in organizing local life. The native central elites who labored to create a unified kingdom were gone, but the more local forms of society were still present. With this lower level of social organization and a thin overlay of imperial bureaucracy at the top, the rest of society's local institutions and some of its regional ones probably remained intact. Family life, cultural traditions, modes of economic productivity, behavioral norms and values, ideological assumptions, and local religious rituals probably were among these cultural constants.[30]

This picture of ongoing life under the Babylonian campaign against Jerusalem is not found in the archaeological remains according to Stern. Stern's research is consistent in revealing that most of Jerusalem and several locations just south of the area, remain devastated until the Persian period. Although he recognizes the possibility of the existence of a small population during the Babylonian period, he is convinced that for the most part, central Judah was uninhabited.

> ...there is virtually no clearly defined period that may be called "Babylonian," for it was a time from which almost no material finds remain. This means that the country was populated, and there were settlements, but that the population was very small in number, and that large parts of the towns and villages were either completely or partly destroyed, and the rest were poorly functioning.... Only two regions appear to have been spared this fate: the northern part of Judah, i.e., the region of Benjamin, which did not

---

[30] Miller and Hayes, 421.

suffer terribly from the Babylonians and exhibits signs of relative prosperity; and probably the land of Ammon, a region that still awaits further investigation.[31]

Religious Status

In 2 Kings 25 and Jeremiah 44 and 52, inter alia, it is declared that the unfaithfulness of the people and the sinfulness of their political leaders are the reasons for the destruction of Judah. But Ezekiel 44 specifies in particular the improper cultic practices of the religious leaders and the abominations against God and the Temple, presumably prior to the destruction of the Temple.

> And say to the rebellious House of Israel: Thus said the Lord God: Too long, O House of Israel, have you committed all your abominations, admitting aliens, uncircumcised of spirit and uncircumcised of flesh, to be in My Sanctuary and profane My very Temple, when you offer up My food - the fat and the blood. Ezek 44:6-7

This text seemingly builds up a case against the people because of their sinfulness and apostasy to God. Still there were many who remained faithful to the religious practices of their ancestors. Perhaps evidence for this can be found in the pilgrimage of the eighty men from Shechem, Shiloh and Samaria, who came to Jerusalem to offer sacrifices after the devastation of the city (Jer 41:5-6). This suggests that Jerusalem was still regarded as the holy place to worship Yahweh, even for many residents of the former northern kingdom.

Many texts address the religious climate after the second deportation. Truly the responses are different. Jer 41:5-6 gives the impression of faithfulness to the Jerusalem site as a special place, perhaps even the only proper place for offering sacrifices to God. But Jer 44:16-18, in the message to those who have escaped to Egypt, presents a mode of despair and conflict where some are insisting that the worship of the Queen of Heaven be reestablished. Taking into consideration the chaos and suffering that Israel is experiencing at this time, both attitudes may make sense. The killing of Gedaliah by Ishmael doubtless was prompted in part by the Davidide status of Ishmael, who felt that Gedaliah's position was that of a traitor. Ishmael himself may have had a hereditary claim to the position

---

[31] Stern, 350.

briefly held by Gedaliah.

However, whether or not sacrifices were made at the ruined temple site is still questionable for many scholars. The Jer 41:5-6 reference is used to argue that sacrifice of some kind remained a part of the cult left in Palestine.[32] But Douglas Jones argues the opposite. He cites Psalms 40, 51, 69 and 102 as evidence that there was no legitimate sacrifice of any kind being performed in Jerusalem.[33] Based on the language of lamentation used in these Psalms, the references to no sacrifice, and the hope of sacrifice resuming sometime in the near future when Zion is restored, Jones makes a convincing argument to support his notion that legitimate sacrifice--at least as understood by the psalmists--ceased from 586 B.C.E., or at least soon thereafter, until the return of the exiles, and the eventual rebuilding of the temple. The language used in the Jer 41:5 text is open for interpretation with the use of the term *mnhh*.[34] Jones argues that this technical term *mnhh* is ambiguous and has been used in pre-exilic times and post-exilic times, but usually in conjunction with other sacrifices.[35] It always seems to suggest a vegetable or grain offering of some kind.

There is not a great deal of direct information about what went on in

---

[32] See R.E. Clements, Jeremiah. (Atlanta: John Knox Press, 1988), p. 233, John Bright, A History of Israel, (Phila: Westminster Press, 1972), 344, Philip James Hyatt, IB, "Jeremiah" (New York:Abingdon Press, 1956), v. 5, 1087-88.

[33] Douglas Jones, "Cessation of Sacrifice After 586 B.C.E.", JOTS, N.S., Vol XIV, Pt. I, April, 1963, 30.

[34] Jones, 15.

[35] Jones, 15.

Judah during the exile. Most of the information available, outside of the biblical texts, is deduced from the period after the exile and the situations that Ezra and Nehemiah faced upon their return almost a century later. The books of Jeremiah and Ezekiel shed some light on the conditions, but for the most part scholars and archaeologists are still trying to put the pieces together.

Archaeological Evidence

Recent archaeological information does not support the argument in favor of a significant population left in Judah after the three deportations. Those who argue in favor of a repopulated Judah again choose not to make a distinction between the northern region of Benjamin and the central region of Jerusalem. This seems to be the case when Amihai Mazar and G. Barkey (Barkai) make the following conclusions in regards to their archaeological excavations.

> However, there is some evidence of a continuation of life at several Judean sites, particularly north of Jerusalem. The most prominent of these is Mizpah (Tel enNasbeh), where occupation was uninterrupted throughout the sixth century B.C.E., corresponding to the biblical account which describes this city as the center of continued Judean autonomy. Similar continuous settlement during the sixth century B.C.E. was also evident at other sites in the region, such as Tell el-Ful (Gibeah), Gibeon, and Bethel, and at the fortress of Khirbet Abu et-Twein in the Hebron hills.[36]

Yet Barkey argues that life continued in the Transjordan, but not necessarily in Jerusalem proper:

> In Transjordan, there was a cultural and habitational continuum from the seventh century to the Persian period. Judea itself was not entirely laid waste; areas that capitulated to the Babylonians before the fall of Jerusalem were spared destruction, especially in the land of Benjamin. Evidence for this was found in excavations at Gibeon, Mizpah (Tell en-Nasbeh), and Bethel, and the governor appointed by the Babylonians resided at Mizpah after the fall of Jerusalem (Jer. 40:9-10).[37]

Archaeological excavations of caves and tombs at Beth Shemesh and Gibeah (Tell el-Ful) have provided much information about the cultural

---

[36] Amihai Mazar, <u>Archaeology of the land of the Bible</u> (New York: Doubleday, 1990), 548.

[37] Barkay, 372.

continuity of Judah after the Exile.[38] The continuity seems clear from the 7th century B.C.E. and through the 6th century B.C.E.[39] This was seen in the pottery of Iron Age III, as well as jewelry and religious figurines.[40] Archaeological evidence, according to Barkai, is in support of the insurrection by Ishmael against Gedaliah and his administration. Barkai summarizes the archaeological evidence in this way:

> Israelite culture, rooted in the Iron Age I, flourished from the tenth century onward under the United Monarchy and the kingdoms of Israel and Judah. As information becomes available from excavations, it may be said that Israelite culture came to an end between 530 B.C.E. and 520 B.C.E.[41]

Stern is in agreement with Berquist, Mazar and Barkay, in regards to the presence of inhabitants in the northern regions of Judah after the exile.

> These finds allow us to assume that the region of Benjamin, with all its major towns, even if partly ruined by the Babylonians in 586 B.C.E. was quickly reconstructed probably becoming a haven for some of the refugees from other parts of Judah. Its major town, Mizpah, even became the temporary capital of the destroyed Judean state. At other towns, particularly Gibeon and Mozah, wine production either continued or was resumed. All these Benjaminite settlements continued to exist during the rest of the Babylonian period.[42]

Stern's position was also argued earlier by S.S. Weinburg in regards to the absence of any significant population left in Jerusalem

> ....excavations by Kathleen Kenyon yield a picture of ruin and desolation that confronted the first returnees of 539/38. While some people had no doubt continued to live in Jerusalem, the archaeological picture is one of their squatting among the rubble, which increased as the terrace walls...collapsed through lack of care and the debris accumulated in impassable piles on the lower slopes. No great change in the condition of the city occurred until the time of Nehemiah's arrival in 445. We must think

---

[38] Barkay, 372.

[39] Barkay, 372.

[40] Barkay, 372.

[41] Barkay, 373.

[42] Stern, 322.

more in terms first of squatters and then of people able to maintain only a mere subsistence level.[43]

Therefore, it seems clear that for the most part, archaeologists agree that Jerusalem was left in ruins and generally unpopulated after the exile. The confusion seems to occur when areas north (i.e. Benjamin), which continued to thrive through the Babylonian Period, are confused with the city of Jerusalem when the geographical area is referred to as "Judah."

The Exiles in Babylon

Textual Evidence

As noted earlier in the chapter, the biblical record points to three deportations to Babylon by king Nebuchadrezzar 598/7, 587/86 and 582 B.C.E. Direct information in regards to the plight of the exiles living in Babylonia is found primarily in the books of Jeremiah, Ezekiel, Psalms, and Deutero-Isaiah. Jer 29:4-7 records advice by the prophet regarding the situation of the people of the first deportation:

> Thus said the Lord of Hosts, the God of Israel, to the whole community which I exiled from Jerusalem to Babylon: Build houses and live in them, plant gardens and eat their fruit. Take wives and beget sons, and give your daughters to husbands, that they may bear sons and daughters. Multiply there, do not decrease. And seek the welfare of the city to which I have exiled you and pray to the Lord in its behalf; for in its prosperity you shall prosper.

Location

Ezekiel 3:15 says the following about the location of the exiles:

> And I came to the exile community that dwelt in Tel Abib by the Chebar Canal, and I remained where they dwelt.

Ezra 2:59 and Neh 7:61 refer to similar sites such as Tel Melah, Tel Harsha, Cherah, Adbon and Immer, as having been inhabited by exiled Jews. The Chebar Canal is a well known watercourse. Thompson states that "Its

---

[43] S.S. Weinburg, "Post-Exilic Palestine: An Archaeological Report", Proceedings of the Israel Academy of Sciences and Humanities 4 (1971), 80-81.

ancient course left the Euphrates River north of Babylon and flowed 60 miles S.E. through the vicinity of ancient Nippur, rejoining the Euphrates south of Warka (biblical Erech)." [44]

Another settlement, Tel Abib, was also near the Chebar. It is along such a canal that perhaps the famous Psalm 137 was uttered by the exiles when requested to sing one of the songs of Zion:

> By the rivers of Babylon, there we sat,
> sat and wept, as we thought of Zion.
> There on the poplars we hung up our lyres,
> for our captors asked us there for songs,
> our tormentors, for amusement,
> "Sing us one of the songs of Zion." (NJPS)

Several settlements are believed to have existed along this watercourse and their large manors and date palm groves provided food and shade.[45] The Chebar Canal is believed to be the modern Shatt el-Nil.[46]

Social and Political Conditions.

Although many of the captives who had been active during the revolt against Nebuchdrezzar were either killed outright or removed in chains, as was the case with Jehoaichin (2 Kgs 25:27) and Zedekiah (2 Kgs 25:7), it seems clear that the exiles, at least for the most part, did not become slaves. Many of the exiles doubtless enjoyed relative freedom of movement, as in the case of Ezekiel, and there seemed to be a limited local government in place, led by the "elders" (Ezek 8:1; 14:1; 20:1,3).[47] Ezra 2:59 and 8:17 suggests that the exiles lived in families or professional groups. Ezra 2:36 suggests that Levites, priests and other former temple officials constituted a particular group. Presumably, some priests and elders also took over the leadership functions and served as a type of self-governing group.[48] Some

---

[44] Henry O. Thompson, "Chebar", in <u>Anchor Bible Dictionary</u>, (New York: Doubleday, 1992), ed. David Noel Freedman, 893.

[45] Thompson, 893.

[46] Thompson, 893.

[47] J. A. Thompson, <u>The Bible and Archaeology</u> (Grand Rapids: Eerdmans, 1989), 189.

[48] Rainer Albertz, <u>A History of Israelite Religion in the Old Testament</u>

evidence for this can be found in the study by E.J. Bickerman, wherein he refers to a cuneiform legal document dated from 529 B.C.E., which mentions an "assembly of elders in Babylon." Bickerman suggests that perhaps a similar assembly existed among the elders in the Judahite colony.[49]

Kaufmann argues that there were various categories of captives among the exiles.

> Among the exiles, there were various categories. There were captives, those who had taken active part in revolt and war, and who were sent into exile in chains and imprisoned. There were those who had been "torn away," those whom the kings of Assyria and Babylon transported ("plucked off") from the homeland in order to weaken and end the strength of the rebellious nation. There were refugees, men who fled their country because of the terrors of war. There were emigrants, men who departed for reasons of family or material well-being. We must distinguish these various categories in order to understand the sources which bear on conditions in the diaspora.[50]

A study by the noted Soviet scholar, M. A. Dandameyev, examined the social and economic conditions of Babylonian society during the 7th-4th centuries B.C.E. Dandameyev found four class levels in Chaldean society:
1) Persons with full civil rights.
2) The Landless class- including free-born persons, both foreign officials and aliens (merchants and craftsmen);
3) Those who were assigned to officials or to royal and temple lands. (They were not slaves that could be bought and sold, but were without civil rights).
4) Slavery proper. There was no evidence found for a large slave class. The economy was not suited to absorb large numbers of slaves.[51]

It would appear, then, in terms of Dandameyev's study, that the

---

[49] Period. (Louisville: Westminster John Knox Press, 1992), 373.
E. J. Bickerman. "The Babylonian Captivity", as cited by Rainer Albertz, A History of Israelite Religion in the Old Testament Period, 599, n.22. footnote # 22.

[50] Yehezkel Kaufmann, The Babylonian Captivity and Deutero-Isaiah, vol IV, chapters 1,2 of History of the Religion of Israel (New York: Union of American Hebrew Congregations, 1970), 5.

[51] Muhammed A. Dandameyev, "A Social Stratification in Babylonian (7th-4th centuries B.C.E.)", in Wirtschaft und Gesellschaft im Alten Vordersaien, Harmatta and Komoroczy, eds. (Budapest, 1976), 98.

majority of the exiles would probably fall under the third class, those assigned to officials or to royal and temple lands, but some may have been part of the landless class.

Oded argues that the exiles experienced "...a certain internal autonomy and that they enjoyed the freedom to manage their community life (Ezek 33:30-33)..."[52] In agreement with Oded, Whitley concludes from then known archaeological and literary evidence, that the exile was "an honorable and easy one."[53] Smith-Christopher disagrees with Oded who argues that the exiles were comparatively well off.[54] According to Smith-Christopher, "Oded believes that there is no evidence of suppression or religious persecution,..."[55] Smith-Christopher objects to such a portrayal of a tame and comfortable lifestyle for the exiles and emphasizes the serious trauma of such an experience, whatever their economic status.

> It is precisely these tendencies to presume a tame, even if not entirely comfortable, existence that needs to be challenged in the light of an analysis informed by the experience of exiles throughout history, and the evidence of trauma in the Hebrew literature after the experience.[56]

Smith-Christopher argues that scholars use the word "slavery" according to their own contexts. For example, when American scholars use the word slavery the context is that of the African-American slaves in ante-bellum United States.[57] Yet the definition must instead come from biblical and nonbiblical texts that refer to the situation at hand. Weissbach analyzed the cuneiform inscription of Nebuchdnezzar II focussing primarily on phrases

---

[52] Bustenay Oded, "Judah and the Exile", Israelite and Judean History, J.M. Miller and J.H. Hayes, eds. (Phila: Westminster, 1986), 483.

[53] Charles Francis Whitley, The Exilic Age (London: Longmans, Green and Co., 1957), 81.

[54] Oded, 435-88.

[55] Daniel Smith-Christopher, "Reassessing the Historical and Sociological Impact of the of the Babylonian Exile 597/587-539 B.C.E.", in Exile: Old Testament, Jewish, and Christian Conceptions, ed James M. Scott. Supplements to the Journal of the Study of Judaism, Vol. 56. (New York: Brill, 1997), 23.

[56] Smith-Christopher, 23

[57] Smith-Christopher, 23.

"I forced them to work on the building of Etemanki" and "I imposed on them the brick-basket..." as indicators of involuntary corvee labor of that period.[58] In his study of social justice practices in ancient Israel, Weinfeld focused on the Akkadian terms used for "labor" - *ilku* and *tupikku*. He concluded that both terms are variants of terms for forced labor, as found also in Hittite and Egyptian nomenclature.[59]

Religious Status

The religious reform under Josiah prohibited sacrifices being offered outside of the Jerusalem temple, and these prohibitions were widely accepted. Therefore, worship and religious practices during the exile were limited. The lack of a central temple gave rise to individual reflections and responses to their situation. Whitley states the following about the worship experience in Babylon.

> The communal worship at the central sanctuary was no longer possible; and although communities governed by elders now met for purposes of prayer, the worship of Yahweh was perforce a matter of the individual conscience. The more, therefore, the individual Israelite was encouraged to think and act for himself, the sooner could he 'make' within him 'a new heart and a new spirit' (Ezek. 18:31) and discover the secret of personal fellowship with God. If, moreover, the religion of Israel were to survive it could only do so through individual exiles.[60]

Rainer Albertz gives this opinion about the worship status of the exiles:

---

[58] F.H. Weissbach, Das Hauptheiligtum des Marduk in Babylon (Leipzig: Hinrichs, 1938), 46.
[59] M. Weinfeld, Social Justice in Ancient Israel and in the Ancient Near East, (Phila: Fortress, 1995), 85.
[60] Whitley, 113-114.

....the main cult of the exilic period was predominantly lamentation.... Thus this occasional form of worship .... not tied to a holy place, became the element which supported the regular main cult in the exilic period.... Even if foreign lands were regarded as cultically unclean (I Sam 26:19; II Kgs 5:17; Jer. 5:19; Ps 137:4), services of lamentation were also possible among the exiles. [61]

Albertz also points out that this type of worship was not restricted to the temple priest, but could be pursued by non-priestly persons.[62] Alfred J. Hoerth states the following in regards to the religious practices of those in exile:

> Of greatest importance, especially to the religious, the exiles were allowed freedom of worship. This privilege can be inferred from the false prophets that Jeremiah's letter also addressed, the repeated access that people had to Ezekiel, and Ezra's later being recognized for his knowledge of the Jewish faith. Also, the synagogue emerged during the Babylonian exile as a replacement for the distant and destroyed temple. Both Ezra and Ezekiel state that study of the law could be an acceptable substitute for sacrifice, and this is what began to take place within synagogues.[63]

Ezekiel 14 and 20 makes reference to the practices of syncretism and idolatry in the exiled community. Nonetheless, we glean from Second Isaiah that many of the exiles were faithful to the Yahwistic tradition and continued to worship Yahweh alone.

Cogan reports on the situation in the following words:

> The weekly Sabbath rest and the covenant of circumcision developed into clear ethnic markers of the exiles. It is just possible that an institution that might be termed a "protosynagogue" took its first steps. At public gatherings on fast days, the exiles lamented the loss of their former homeland and prayed for a speedy return. On such occasions the

---

[61] Albertz, 377.

[62] Albertz, 377.

[63] Alfred J. Hoerth, Archaeology and the Old Testament, (Grand Rapids:Baker Fall of Babylon", The Oxford History of the Biblical World, Michael D. Coogan, ed. (Oxford: Oxford University Press, 1998), 271.

[63] James Wellard, By the Waters of Babylon (London: Hutchinson and Co, 1972), 177.

[63] Miller and Hayes, 434.Books, 1998), 385.

teaching of prophets and the reading of sacred texts from preexilic times may also have filled the spiritual void.[64]

In light of the exiles' ability to maintain their religious and moral traditions during their existence in Babylonia, Wellard concludes that "What is certain is that the Israelites, alone of the conquered people, kept alive their religious and moral traditions throughout the period of exile, and they could only have done this if the Babylonian authorities had allowed them to live as a privileged group among the thousands of other prisoners of wars from all over the empire."[65]

Although there is no direct evidence, scholars have concluded the following about worship experiences in Babylon:

> The exiles probably worshiped in a nonsacrificial cult in which prayer, praise, and reading and exposition of the law were characteristic. Sermons, such as those found in Ezekiel and the prose passages of Jeremiah, were perhaps commonplace. This type of worship could function anywhere, requiring only a meeting place (*synagogue* in Greek). [66]

Archaeological Evidence

Archaeological evidence revealing the presence of the exiles in Babylon is limited. The nearest site presumably connected to the exiles is a region called the river or canal Chebar, mentioned above. This location is about sixty miles southeast of Babylon. There is clear textual evidence that there were Jews living in this area sometime around 500-400 B.C.E., a group believed to be descendants of the exilic community. [67]

Although at least some of those who were taken in the first deportation were settled in the region along the Chebar, much of the evidence from cuneiform documents (the Mura_hu Archives), comes from the ancient site of Nippur in southern Mesopotamia, near the Chebar. Villages of exiles on the Chebar River near Nippur include: Tel-abib, Tel-melah, Tel-harsha,

---

[64] Mordechai Cogan, "Into Exile: From the Assyrian Conquest of Israel to the Fall of Babylon", The Oxford History of the Biblical World, Michael D. Coogan, ed. (Oxford: Oxford University Press, 1998), 271.

[65] James Wellard, By the Waters of Babylon (London: Hutchinson and Co, 1972), 177.

[66] Miller and Hayes, 434.

[67] J.A. Thompson, 189.

Cherub, Addan, Immer and Casphia.[68] For an earlier time, clay tablets discovered in Babylon indicate a rise in status for the king in exile, with the rations of oil, barley and other food given to King Jehoiachin and his entourage.[69] Economic, administrative and literary documents illustrating the Chaldean society and how it related to foreigners and persons placed in exile may also shed some light on this period as well. Business documents from the 5th century B.C.E., such as the Murashu documents, suggest that perhaps the Jewish exiles were by that time experiencing some level of prosperity even in exile. Coogan makes the following conclusions in regards to the link between the Murashu documents and West Semitic names.

> We presume that individuals with Yahwistic names (i.e., names in *yahu* or *yaw*) are Jewish. Although it is possible that some Aramaeans or even Babylonians may have adopted these theophorous elements in the names of their children, we do not think it likely. Names in -*yaw* do not occur in Neo-Babylonian sources before the Exile, and their increasing frequency in the late sixth and fifth centuries can reasonably be associated with the gradual emancipation and increased prosperity of Judeaean exiles in Mesopotamia.[70]

The Egyptian Gola
The Biblical Evidence

After the murder of Gedaliah, some survivors made an escape to Egypt in fear of retaliation from King Nebuchdrezzar. Although Jeremiah counseled against the remnant going to Egypt to seek refuge, the remnant voted to ignore Jeremiah's advice and journeyed to Egypt, taking Jeremiah and Baruch along with them:

> So Johanan son of Kareah and all the army officers and the rest of the people did not obey the Lord's command to remain in the land of Judah. Instead, Johanan son of Kareah and all the army officers took the entire remnant of Judah - those who had returned from all the countries to which they had been scattered and had sojourned in the land of Judah, men,

---

[68] Yohanan Aharoni, Michael Avi-Yonah, Anson F. Rainey, Safrai Ze'ev. The Macmillan Bible Atlas, (New York: Macmillan, 1993), 3rd edition, 125.

[69] James B. Pritchard, Ancient Near Eastern Texts Relating to the Old Testament (Princeton: Princeton University Press, 1969), 308.

[70] Michael D. Coogan, West Semitic Personal Names in the Murašû Documents, (Missoula: Scholars Press, 1976), 119.

women, and children; and the daughters of the king and all the people whom Nebuzaradan the chief of the guards had left with Gedaliah son of Ahikam son of Shaphan, as well as the prophet Jeremiah and Baruch son of Neriah - and they went to Egypt. They did not obey the Lord. Jer. 43:4-7

In 2 Kings 25:26 and Jeremiah 43- 44 we find the only biblical accounts of this Egyptian Gola. Then in Jer 44:11-14 we find a prophecy that projects the fate of those who fled to Egypt:

> Of all the remnant of Judah who came to sojourn here in the land of Egypt, no survivor or fugitive shall be left to return to the land of Judah. Though they all long to return and dwell there, none shall return except (a few) survivors. Jer 44:14

Therefore, in addition to exiles in Babylonia and some people in the area of Benjamin, there apparently was at least a small community in Egypt.

Religious Status

Cogan states the following in regards to the situation in Egypt for the escaped exiles.

> Nothing is known of this southern Diaspora scattered about Egypt, save for the small community at Elephantine, an island in the Nile just north of the First Cataract, near modern Aswan. A collection of Aramaic ostraca and papyri dating from the end of the fifth century B.C.E. discovered on the island contains the records of a military garrison of Judeans in the employ of the Persians. In addition to legal deeds concerning the private affairs of individuals (marriage and divorce, sales and purchases), a memorandum discussing the proper observance of the Passover and the Festival of Unleavened Bread is of particular note. Unlike their formal compatriots in Babylonia, however, the Judeans at Elephantine served the God of Israel at a temple where animal sacrifices were offered, and there is also some evidence that they reverenced Aramean deities. Yet this significant difference in religious practice did not alienate them from the leaders in Judah and Samaria, to whom they appealed to intercede on their behalf before the Persian authorities concerning the reconstruction of their house of worship. Still, the ex-Judeans at Elephantine were passed over by history until their rediscovery in modern times, when their affairs were reconstructed as an exotic footnote.[71]

Cogan concurs with Steinmann who earlier states that the Elephantine community was already in place by the 6th century when Cambyses

---

[71] Cogan, 272.

conquered Egypt.

> On ne sait rien de ce qui s'est alors passé dans le Delta. En revanche, on est bien renseigné par les papyri d'Élephantine sur une colonie juive de Haute Égypte. Certains de ces papyri datent de la quatorzième année de Darius, donc d'un siècle plus tard. Mais ils font allusion à une situation antérieure. Le temple à Yaho, que détruisirent les prêtres égyptiens du dieu Chnoub, était déjà édifié au temps de la conquête de l'Égypt par Cambyse au VI siécle. Et le Père Lagrange estimait "qu'n'y aurait rien d'ètonnant à ce que les Juifs d'Éléphantine soient demeurés au point où l'on en était en Judée, avant la réforme de Josias". En effet ces Juifs n'éprouvent aucun scrupule à édifier un temple à Iahvé en terre pâïenne. Ils y pratiquent une religion archaïque et populaire, avec ses fêtes, en particulier la Pâque. Ils offrent des sacrifices à Iahvé, sans tenir compte du *Deutéronome*, qui n'allait entrer dans les moeurs des Juifs qu'au retour de l'Exil.[72]

Archaeological Evidence

Jeremiah 43 tells us that a remnant from Judah, led by Johanan and Azariah, arrived at Tahpanhes, an Egyptian outpost in the eastern delta of Egypt bordering Sinai.[73] Here Jeremiah received a word from the Lord and he was told to "take large stones and place them in the mortar in the brick structure at the entrance to Pharoah's palace in Tahpanhes" (43:9). (This was symbolic of the attack that King Nebuchadrezzar was to forge against Egypt. In this attack, as forecast, Nebuchadrezzar would burn down the temples of the gods of Egypt).

The site that is believed to be the ancient Tahpanhes is Tell ed-Defenneh. It is located "about 8 km W of el-Qantara and about 24 km SW of Pelusium/Farmea/Tell el-Farama".[74] This site was discovered by Sir Flinders Petrie in 1887. In his excavations he found pottery, weaponry and various other artifacts dated to the periods covering 609-566 B.C.E.[75]

In ANET, there is a memorandum written by Bagoas, the Persian

---

[72] Jean Steinmann, Le Livre de La Consolation D'Israël et Les Prophètes Du Retour De L'Exil, Lectio Divina 28 (Paris: Les Éditions Du Cerf, 1960), 71-72.

[73] Richard N. Jones and Zbugbuew T. Fiema, "Tahpanhes", Anchor Bible Dictionary Vol. 5, (New York: Doubleday, 1992), David Noel Freedman, ed., 308.

[74] Jones and Fiema, 308.

[75] Jones and Fiema, 308.

governor of Judah and Delaiah, governor of Samaria that discusses the rebuilding of the temple at Elephantine.[76] The memorandum gives a directive to the governor of Judah "to build it on its site as it was before, and the meal-offering and incense to be made on the altar as it used to be."[77]

Additional evidence indicates a Jewish military community on the southern Egyptian island of Elephantine by the beginning of the 5th century. Evidence was found there in the form of papyrus documents written in Aramaic by a colony of Jews in the period of 500-400 B.C.E.[78] One of the letters was addressed to the Persian governor of Jerusalem in the year 407-408 B.C.E. This letter asked permission to rebuild a temple on Elephantine. Scholars dispute as to whether or not those who wrote these documents were direct descendants of the Egyptian Gola of 586 B.C.E.

Miller and Hayes observed several characteristics of the Jewish migration to Egypt in their review of the Elephantine archives (see ANET 491-92, 548-49). They listed eight interesting features about the *social, political and religious* life in the Egyptian Gola:

1) The Elephantine community was a small military colony which included women and children.
2) There was intermarriage with Egyptians and assimilation in both directions.
3) Some Jewish persons rose to high positions in local administrative matters and some accumulated significant wealth.
4) The community retained contact with the religious authorities in both Jerusalem and Samaria.
5) The colony possessed limited internal autonomy and governed itself according to the customs of their ancestors.
6) The community was at least aware of many traditional Jewish practices, including observance of the Sabbath, and such festivals as Passover and Unleavened Bread.
7) They possessed a temple that bore structural similarity to the one in Jerusalem, and in which the ancestral god Yahweh was worshiped and sacrifices were offered.
8) Indications suggest that the Jews at Elephantine were

---

[76] Edwin M. Yamauchi, Persia and the Bible (Grand Rapids: Baker Books, 1990), 91.

[77] ANET, 91.

[78] Jones and Fiema, 308.

syncretistic in their worship.[79] (See also Jer 44:8)

Summary

As has been demonstrated in this chapter, the "Sitz im Leben" of the Jews during the Exile and after the three deportations, were varied. There were some people left in the land to carry on, especially in the Benjaminite area. There were thousands of people taken into captivity and forced to live in Babylon. Then there were also those who chose to leave Judah and go down to Egypt--and perhaps to other neighboring nations--for refuge and security against Nebuchdrezzar's military campaigns. These were all a potential audience for a message of hope and comfort. This message was to come in the period 550/546 to 539 B.C.E., from a prophet known as Deutero-Isaiah. He was called forth to announce a new thing God was about to do. Although his audiences were varied and although they experienced different situations and circumstances, Deutero-Isaiah's message could potentially include all accessible audiences as known from the Biblical and archaeological tradition. To examine this situation, we turn now to the indicators in Isaiah 40-55.

---

[79] Miller and Hayes, 435.

CHAPTER 2

THE AUDIENCE(S) OF DEUTERO-ISAIAH THE SCHOLARS' OPINIONS

Most scholars agree that Deutero-Isaiah is exilic. However, scholars differ on just who is addressed in chapters 40-55. The text mentions by name several possible audiences. They include two common parallelisms: Jacob/Israel (40:27; 41:8, 14; 42:24;43:1,22; 44:1,2,21;44:23; 45:4; 46:3; 48:1,12) and Zion/Jerusalem (40:9; 41:27; 46:13; 49:14; 51:3, 11, 17; 52:2,9). Also specified are Babylon (47), coast lands/nations (41:1; 42:10; 45:20; 48:14; 49:1, 7) and Cyrus (45:1). The chapters feature frequent imperatives suggesting that an immediate audience--either direct or indirect--is meant to hear these words. The speakers vary as well. There appears to be three main speakers throughout the chapters: God (40-45, 50-51); the prophet (40:27; 42:13,24; 44:1-5; 48:20); and the servant (49:1-6; 50:4-11) along with other unidentified voices (40:3,6-23; 53). The dating of Deutero-Isaiah also varies according to the commentaries. The dates include a primary range from passages as early as ca 550 B.C.E. (Westermann) to passages as late as 450 B.C.E. (Torrey, Baltzer, Watts) and 400 B.C.E. (U.E. Simon).

This chapter will present the opinions of seven recent commentaries in regards to who is addressed in these chapters. The seven scholars are: Claus Westermann, George A.F. Knight, R.N. Whybray, Richard Clifford, Paul Hanson, Walter Brueggemann, and Klaus Baltzer. In addition to these seven major commentators, reference will be made to interpretations of Norman K. Gottwald, Robert P. Carroll, Robert Wilson and Daniel Smith-Christopher.

There are three basic underlying perspectives found throughout this chapter. The first perspective is that the major audience of Deutero-Isaiah is the exiles. Although other audiences are mentioned, it will become clear that those in exile are the primary focus and are addressed as the "true servant" Israel. The second perspective is that the city of Jerusalem is in ruins and any Judeans who remained in Judah are viewed as an insignificant audience and are only addressed in connection with the return of the exiles. Most of the commentators either ignore a presence in Judah or they assign the residents in a minor role. The third perspective is the necessity for the message of salvation to come from Zion/Jerusalem, which is viewed as the unique place from which the presence and power of God will become known to the whole world. The central features of divine comfort are the emphasis on the return of the exiles, the task to be carried out from Zion/Jerusalem, and the encompassing of scattered Israel as well as the nations. This divine comfort can only be fully experienced by those back in Jerusalem who carry out the Servant's true task.

Analysis of the Audiences
Claus Westermann

Westermann dates the writing of Deutero-Isaiah "some time after 550 B.C.E., the year which saw the beginning of the victorious campaign of Cyrus."[80] In an effort to discern the true audiences within these chapters, Westermann uses genre as a major key to unlocking the identity of the audience(s). Yet, for Westermann, it is clear that the entire nation is addressed, those left in Judah and those taken into exile. He discusses each audience and offers an explanation for the role they are expected to play in Deutero-Isaiah's thought as well as their function in proclaiming God's message to all the world.

Jacob/Israel

Westermann argues that Deutero-Isaiah refers to Israel as a nation primarily as "Jacob/Israel" (40:27; 41:8; 42:24; 43:1, 22,28; 44:21,22; 45:4; 46:3; 48:1,12; 49:6).

Westermann identifies this audience through the use of appositions that describe the relationship between Israel and God.

> But you, Israel, my servant,
> You, Jacob, whom I have chosen.
> 41:8; 44:1

For Westermann code phrases such as "my servant" and "whom I have chosen" refer to Israel's past when God called her out of Egypt.[81] Israel was then one united people and Westermann interprets Deutero-Isaiah's frequent use of these code phrases as evidence that the audience is both those in exile and those left in Judah. Westermann also recognizes the use of the apposition "who created you," and "...and formed you" as code

---

[80] Claus Westermann, Isaiah 40-66. (Westminster Press:Philadelphia, 1969), 5.

[81] Westermann, 69.

phrases that support the identity of the parallelism "Jacob/Israel" as the whole nation: (43:1)

> Jacob....Israel referred strictly to Israel the nation, the words can only mean, 'who created you as a nation...' the creating and forming refer to an actual historical act of God. [82]

Therefore, in Westermann's opinion the primary audience of Deutero-Isaiah is the entire nation.

> The audience addressed by the prophet is the entire nation taken as a unit; never-the- less, the word of God given him to proclaim is meant to affect every individual member at the most personal and existential level. [83]

Yet, even after making this statement, Westermann acknowledges that those in exile are in the forefront of Deutero-Isaiah's mind. He says the following in regards to 52:2: "the people whom the prophet has chiefly in mind are the exiles."[84]

Although Westermann maintains the position that Deutero-Isaiah always ultimately addresses Israel as a whole nation, he states that in some instances Deutero-Isaiah focused more intentionally on a particular segment of his audience in order to make his point more clear. So at times Westermann identifies the exiles as the primary audience. This can be seen in several texts (42:10-13; 46:3-4; 45:9-11; 48:20, 21; 49:1-4) . Westermann states the following in his interpretation of 46:3-4.

> The voice.... turns to the exiles (46:3-4). They are addressed as "remnants of the house of Israel," being thus reminded of the catastrophic events from which they had escaped. [85]

Zion/Jerusalem

A second important audience parallelism in Deutero-Isaiah is "Zion/Jerusalem." Although the parallelism uses a specific location, thus suggesting an audience actually in Jerusalem, for Westermann, the

---

[82] Westermann, 117.

[83] Westermann, 13.

[84] Westermann, 247.

[85] Westermann, 180.

parallelism seems to refer to the exiles as those about to return to Jerusalem, whence they came. Westermann finds this double address used when Deutero-Isaiah is announcing the return of God and the people to Judah. This suggests that those left behind in Judah are ignored. Westermann says the following in regards to 52:1-2.

> Although it is "Zion...Jerusalem" that is actually addressed as captive in v. 2a, b, the people who Deutero-Isaiah has chiefly in mind are the exiles - he often gives them the name Zion..... The loosing of the bonds does not relate to the city but to the exiles.[86]

Other Audiences

Westermann recognizes two additional audiences - the nations/coast lands and the servant (who may or may not be Israel as a whole nation). However, neither of these two audiences is addressed as frequently as the parallelisms "Jacob/Israel" and "Zion/Jerusalem."

When addressing the nations, Westermann argues that Deutero-Isaiah employs the genres trial speech, hymn of praise and disputation. Again the goal is to convince and persuade the people to accept the new word of salvation from God. The trial speech and the disputation are intended to prove the sovereignty of their God over against the nothingness of gods who are mere idols made of wood. The hymn of praise is used to encourage the victory and success of the message as it achieves the purpose of bringing Israel back to God and announcing God's return to Jerusalem. It is used to call forth the audience from all corners of the earth. It functions also as an invitation to inclusivity

> .....the prophet here proclaims as binding that God's final saving act towards his people is to take place in full view of the entire world of men and of nature, and that it looks for the response not merely of the faithful, but of all men and of nature.[87]

It does not appear that Westermann considers those left in Judah a major audience. He does not develop an argument supporting the presence of people left in Judah, although he states that "Deutero-Isaiah's message is certainly always addressed to the nation taken all together..."[88] Westermann

---

[86] Westermann, 247.

[87] Westermann, 104.

[88] Westermann, 13.

assumes their inclusion within the community laments (51:9-52:3).[89] Judah, the place, is the final destination for Deutero-Isaiah. However, for Westermann it is important to the prophet that Israel move from Babylonia to Jerusalem, the proper place from which they can give witness to the message of salvation and from which they can activate the plan of comfort (40:1-11; 52:7-9).

R.N. Whybray

Whybray dates the corpus of Deutero-Isaiah between 550-538 B.C.E. He bases this dating on the absence of any suggestion of the horrors of the destruction of Jerusalem in the minds of the audience, and of any specific mention of the fall of Babylon. He also argues that Deutero-Isaiah seems to already regard Cyrus as a great conqueror, which could only be assumed after the conquest of the Median Empire and Lydia which took

---

[89] Westermann, 245.

place in 547-46 B.C.E. [90]

Whybray also emphasizes the role of the literary genres in Deutero-Isaiah. Like Westermann, he connects the genres with the audience. [91] Whybray recognizes several audiences in Deutero-Isaiah: the exiles, Zion/Jerusalem, Jacob/Israel, the nations/coast lands, and the servant. However, he presents the exiles as the primary audience and gives very little attention to those who remained in Judah.

The Exiles

For Whybray, the exiles are the primary audience in Deutero-Isaiah. Whybray assumes Isa 40-55 as "...the work of a single prophet, addressed to a group of his fellow-exiles from Jerusalem who are bitterly complaining of their fate at the hands of the Babylonians..."[92]

Whybray argues that Deutero-Isaiah's message is developed to address the exiles. It is a message that focussed on the restoration, independence and prosperity of the Jewish exiles.[93] Whybray goes so far as to interpret every metaphor and parallelism as part of Deutero-Isaiah's strategy to persuade the exiles to remain faithful to God and to their unique relationship and history with God. God had not forsaken them. In Whybray's opinion, "It was not enough for Deutero-Isaiah to assert that Yahweh was about to

---

[90] R.N. Whybray, Isaiah 40-66, (Eerdmans: Grand Rapids, 1975), 22-23.

[91] Whybray, 29.

[92] Whybray, 21.

[93] Whybray, 30.

intervene to rescue the exiles ....he needed to marshall powerful arguments if he was to be believed."[94]

Deutero-Isaiah is creative in addressing the audience of the exiles. According to Whybray, Deutero-Isaiah uses phrases like "your redeemer" that give the impression that the exiles are the intended audience.

> Your redeemer - in using this word of Yahweh's relationship to Israel the prophet seeks to encourage the exiles in two ways: he suggests that Yahweh considers himself under an obligation to help them, an obligation which he will not break ....and that Yahweh's relationship with them is so intimate that he can be described ....as a near kinsmen.[95]

Whybray continues to find evidence which promotes the exiles as a major audience for Deutero-Isaiah. The genre of hymn of praise found in 41:16 suggests the return home of the exiles. It is promised that this return will be the opposite of their deportation. Whybray states that "the final promise is that the exiles on their return home after the removal of all obstacles will sing a song of praise or thanksgiving."[96]

The laments found in Deutero-Isaiah also point to the exiles as the intended audience. Whybray views the complaints recorded in Deutero-Isaiah as one example of how the prophet identifies the exiles as the audience. Then in regard to 42:18-25, Whybray argues that the exiles are those whom Deutero Isaiah refers to as "deaf and blind." They are "deaf and blind" because they "have have reproached Yahweh with being deaf and blind to their fate, but he turns the reproach against them. They are deaf and blind in that they failed to understand the cause of their present miserable situation..."[97]

Again Whybray argues that Deutero-Isaiah uses the metaphor "deaf and blind" to describe the exiles. Despite their spiritual handicap, they are called to be witnesses. In Whybray's analysis of this verse, Deutero-Isaiah holds the exiles responsible for what they have seen despite their affliction of being "deaf and blind". For Whybray then, "in spite of their inability to understand much of what Yahweh has done and is doing, they at least have eyes and have ears sufficiently acute to enable them to act as his

---

[94] Whybray, 53.

[95] Whybray, 65.

[96] Whybray, 66.

[97] Whybray, 79.

witnesses."[98]

Sometimes Deutero-Isaiah makes it appear as if one audience is addressed when in actuality another audience is intended to receive the message. This is often the case when the exiles are addressed. Whybray states the following about chapter 45.

> ...the real audience is the exilic community throughout: the supposed address to Cyrus is a literary fiction similar to the speeches made by Yahweh to the heathen gods and their worshipers in the trial scenes...of all the oracles concerning Cyrus this is the most explicit and the one most calculated to astonish the exiles....[99]

For Whybray, chapter 47 follows the same pattern.

> Babylon's wickedness will lead to her misfortune...but the thought of God's all-seeing eye, a commonplace of the literature of the ancient Near East as well as of Israel, lies in the background as an encouragement to the Jewish exiles: Yahweh may appear to be oblivious of their wrongs, but events will soon show that he has missed nothing.[100]

There appear to be several sub-groups among the exiles who are addressed based on their particular grievance against the servant or the prophet himself. This is apparent in 50:10-11 and 51:1-3. Whybray puts the sub-groups into two categories.

> The two yous are contrasted: in verse 10 it is the faithful exiles who are addressed and exhorted to find their salvation in obedience to Yahweh's Servant, that is, the prophet; in verse 11 those addressed are the Servant's persecutors.[101]

> ...(51:1-3) this oracle is addressed to those among the exiles who have remained faithful to Yahweh but are nevertheless discouraged.[102]

---

[98] Whybray, 84.

[99] Whybray, 103.

[100] Whybray, 123.

[101] Whybray, 153.

[102] Whybray, 155.

God Comforts Israel

It appears that the exiles are a major focus for Deutero-Isaiah according to Whybray. However, Whybray also recognizes other audiences that are directly mentioned in the text. These mentioned groups are sometimes code words for the exiles in conjunction with the city of Jerusalem and/or the whole nation Israel.

Zion/Jerusalem

According to Whybray the parallelism "Zion/Jerusalem" refers both to the exiles and to the city more as a place than as a population. The parallelism is first used in 40:9-11. When Whybray analyzes Deutero-Isaiah he notices that "...it is characteristic of him to oscillate between the two meanings of Zion/Jerusalem - the exiles who longed to return and the city itself." [103] The parallelism is used again in 41:27; 52:1 and (although in a different configuration) 52:7-9. Whybray states that the parallelism refers to both the exiles and the city, yet he admits that from chapter 51 on "Zion/Jerusalem" is portrayed primarily as the city.[104]

The terms "Zion" and "Jerusalem" are also used separately throughout the text (Jerusalem--40:2; 44:6, 28; 51:17; 52:9, Zion--46:13; 49:14; 51:3,11,16; 52:8). In some instances, Whybray argues that "Jerusalem" refers to the exiles. He says the following in regards to 40:1-8.

> In vv 1-2, then, one heavenly being informs others that God is commanding them to comfort the Jewish exiles with the news that the time of their suffering is at an end...Jerusalem (also Zion) is often used by Deutero-Isaiah to designate the exiles rather than the actual city....that it should be used of a people no longer resident in their city shows the intensity of their identification with their home.[105]

In Whybray's analysis of 49:14-23, where "Zion" is used alone, he states that the audience is the city. Here Zion is lamenting over her condition and accusing God of abandoning her.

But Zion said, 'the Lord has forsaken me,
The Lord has forgotten me.'

Whybray continues to identify "Zion" with the city whenever the context

---

[103] Whybray, 52.

[104] Whybray, 163.

[105] Whybray, 48-49.

suggests a place or space to return to (49:17-26). In addition, "Zion" must also receive all her children from the many deportations and exiles, not just from Babylonia. When "Zion" opens her gates, "The population of the city will be greater than ever before, because the returning Israelites will include not only the descendants of the Babylonian exiles but the descendants of dispersed Israelites of all kinds gathered from many countries."[106] Whybray's analysis of this all inclusive welcome home is congruent with the broad metaphor Deutero-Isaiah has for the term Zion, as identified by Whybray. According to Whybray "Zion is for Deutero-Isaiah both the city and the whole nation: the rightful occupants of the whole land, not only of one city."[107] For Whybray, 49:22-23 are a response to Zion's earlier questions (49:21). In Deutero-Isaiah's attempt to respond to these questions, it is announced that "the Israelites dispersed all over the world will be gathered and will return home, with their former oppressors attending them as their slaves."[108]

Jacob/Israel

The parallelism "Jacob/Israel," for Whybray, is another code phrase for the exiles. Whybray calls "Jacob/ Israel" "the complainants" in 40:27 and argues that "this does not mean that God is unable to see the fate (way) of the exiles but that he has deliberately refused to do so."[109] It is Whybray's position that the parallelism "Jacob/Israel" denotes a special status for the exiles. It is God's way of reassuring his people of their special status as his chosen people.

> (Yahweh) seeks to reassure his people, addressing them with a series of epithets which reminds them of their special status as his chosen people and assures them that this has not changed. This assurance is already conveyed by the words Israel/Jacob, and is made more explicit by the phrases, 'my servant' and 'whom I have chosen'.[110]

The parallelism is addressed with a negative note in 41:14-16.

---

[106] Whybray, 145.

[107] Whybray, 145.

[108] Whybray, 146.

[109] Whybray, 58.

[110] Whybray, 63.

> Do not be afraid, O worm Jacob,
> O little Israel.

Whybray again finds these words to be addressed to the exiles and says that both words -- "worm" and "little" are contemptuous, "and are almost certainly used here because the exiles have so described themselves in a lamentation to which this oracle is the reply."[111]

The parallelism changes again in 48:1.

> Listen to this, O house of Jacob,
> You who are called by the name of Israel.
> And come from the line of Judah,
> You who take oaths in the name of the Lord
> and invoke the God of Israel,
> the Lord Almighty is his name.

Here, Deutero-Isaiah uses several appositions to describe the audience. In this context, Whybray argues that Deutero-Isaiah is attempting to address all Israel. Whybray views the trio Jacob/Israel/Judah as the prophet trying "to make it clear that the whole of the former nation of Israel and not merely the Judeans is involved in what he has to say." [112]

The final occurance of the parallelism "Jacob/Israel" is also addressed to the exiles.

> Listen to me, O Jacob,
> Israel, whom I have called:
> I am he;
> I am the first and I am the last. (48:12)

---

[111] Whybray, 65.

[112] Whybray, 127.

Whybray argues that the prophet is portraying God as defending his decision to send Cyrus as the deliverer. God uses the disputation and "as the speaker, seeks to overcome the exiles' doubts about the mission of Cyrus by arguing from the common ground of his limitless power and purpose already demonstrated in the creation of the world and the call of Israel." [113]

In sum, Whybray places great emphasis on the exiles as a major audience in Deutero-Isaiah. However, like Westermann, Whybray acknowledges the presence of other audiences and the strategy of Deutero-Isaiah in oscillating between identities. Unlike Westermann, Whybray interprets the parallelism "Jacob/Israel" more often as referring to the exiles, rather than the whole nation. In addition, Whybray says very little about the audience back in Judah. The people remaining in Judah do not appear to be significant for Whybray's understanding of Deutero-Isaiah's message of comfort. Yet Westermann envisions the whole nation - both the Judahites and the exiles - as the ultimate recipients of Deutero-Isaiah's message of comfort.

Whybray also differs from Westermann in his analysis of the identity of "Zion/ Jerusalem." Whybray finds that the parallelism more often then not refers to the city, the place and the space where the salvation and comfort are to take place. Westermann tends to view the parallelism as one way Deutero-Isaiah places focus on those in exile. Both scholars argue that the return to Jerusalem, the Holy city, is the final destination. It is there that Israel must give witness to the total sovereignty of God. Both scholars depend on the literary genre as crucial to revealing the intent of the author, Westermann more so than Whybray. Whybray disagrees with Westermann's assessment that the literary organization is well done. He concludes that the work is full of editors trying to create a single effort but failing to pull it off.

George A.F. Knight

Knight dates Isaiah 40-55 somewhere between 545 and 540 B.C.E.[114] Knight takes a different approach than Westermann and Whybray in that he states from the outset that Deutero-Isaiah's intention is to focus on the theological thread that turns these closely knit chapters into a developing thesis. [115] Knight agrees with Westermann that chapters 40-55 are a unit. In

---

[113] Whybray, 131.

[114] George A.F. Knight, Isaiah 40-55, Servant Theology (Eerdmans:Grand Rapids, 1984), 13.

[115] Knight, 2.

Knight's opinion, Deutero-Isaiah's "method is to make constant reference backward and forward as he proceeds and bit by bit he binds his book together in one sustained and developing argument." [116] Since Knight's focus is from a theological perspective he admits that he generally depends on the work of the critical scholars.[117]

Knight finds that the exiles are the primary audience in Deutero-Isaiah. Throughout his commentary he identifies the audience as those in Babylonian exile. Although he does recognize a continuing presence in Judah and includes those scattered "to the ends of the earth" in Deutero-Isaiah's audience, it is the depressed exiles carted off in 587 B.C.E. whom the prophet felt were on the brink of total apostasy, and whom he had most in mind. Knight states the following in regards to their spiritual and emotion condition.

---

[116] Knight, 25.

[117] Knight, 3.

Thus it is likely that very few of Deutero-Isaiah's present hearers would even remember the events of 587 B.C.E. when Jerusalem was destroyed. Most of those who had gone into exile in that year would now be dead. Those who were still alive must have had little hope of finding any meaning in their remaining unhappy years. [118]

Knight's perspective on each audience and its importance in Deutero-Isaiah's thought offers some interesting insights and suggestions.

Judah

Knight recognizes those left in Judah as a part of the audience included in the messages given to Israel. Knight agrees with the account found in 2 Kings 25 which records that "not all the people of Judah had been removed to Babylon by Nebuchdrezzar in 587 B.C.E. Many peasants had been left to continue their simple and brutish life in the hill country of the little area known as Judah, then part of a province of the Babylonian Empire." [119] Archaeological evidence to date does not support the presence of any major group of people during this time in Jerusalem (cf. Ephraim Stern, cited above). However, Knight argues that even though the evidence suggests that "the country districts of Judah were at that time terribly decimated and impoverished....Yet these poor folk were also God's people and so were still one with the exiles to whom the angelic message....was now being addressed." [120] Knight insists that those left in Judah were an audience and that Deutero-Isaiah includes them in his message of comfort. In his opinion, "the people of Judah...were to be the first to hear the good news. The remnant, now in Babylon, was to shout it to them the moment they succeeded in getting home to Judah." [121]

Again he advocates for the Judahites as an audience in 41:17-18. Knight argues that "we are told who the poor and needy are. Certainly in the first place they comprise crestfallen Israel in exile. But they also comprise the destitute cities of Judah, whose people had survived in poverty since the fall of the state in 587 B.C.E..." [122]

---

[118] Knight, 74.

[119] Knight, 15.

[120] Knight, 15.

[121] Knight, 15.

[122] Knight, 38.

Knight does not abandon the idea that there is an audience in Judah. In 52:8 he argues that those in Judah are being addressed. Although the city is in ruins, "the people of God who are still living within the ruins now stand up 'all eyes' as the phrase seems to mean, and watch for the very presence of God himself."[123]

Zion/Jerusalem

Unlike Westermann and Whybray, Knight prefers to interpret the meaning and identity of the parallelism "Zion/Jerusalem" separately. Knight relies heavily on the parsing form of the direct object and the immediate context to reveal the intended audience. For example, in 40:2 Israel is addressed as Jerusalem. Knight argues that this reference is a symbol for the people in exile.

> In 40:2, Israel is addressed as Jerusalem. The city of course symbolized the people, even though the latter are presently some 700 miles from home and the walls of the city are lying in ruins. But this figurative use of the word Jerusalem is important in the context of Deutero-Isaiah's exposition. Jerusalem was regarded as a feminine entity...Deutero-Isaiah employs this figure consistently when he has in mind to speak of the people of God as Yahweh's bride.[124]

Knight interprets the "Zion/Jerusalem" parallelism found in 40:9 as follows.

> Consequently Jerusalem dare not keep it to herself. At the moment of speaking Zion - God's people - is dwelling on the flat Mesopotamian plain. But Jerusalem, the ancient capital city of the exiles, straddles a ridge...So the people of God is to get back somehow to Zion and climb on to the top of its high hill....[125]

So here we have "Zion" defined as "God's people" and "Jerusalem" as the physical city. Knight argues that when Israel is referred to in the feminine singular, Deutero-Isaiah chooses to use the terms "Zion" or "Jerusalem."[126] In addition, this feminine connotation is meant to portray

---

[123] Knight, 163.

[124] Knight, 10.

[125] Knight, 15.

[126] Knight, 15.

"Zion" and/or "Jerusalem" as the "bride of Yahweh" (cf 52:1). For Knight, Yahweh's true bride is the exiles in Babylon.[127] This is an image we shall encounter later with other scholars as well (e.g. Baltzer).[128] But for Knight the parallelism "Zion/Jerusalem" includes more than just the city of Jerusalem. He states that "included in Zion's constituency are naturally the small towns and villages of Judah.[129] Knight uses the singular/plural and masculine/feminine forms to help identify the intended audience in 45:14. Here he acknowledges that the "you" is feminine singular (and is repeated five times). Knight identifies the audience as "Jerusalem" for this reason.[130] We find "Zion" referred to in the feminine singular again in 49:14.

> But Zion said, 'the Lord has forsaken me,
> My Lord has forgotten me.'

When Zion is used with the plural "you" in 50:1, Knight identifies the audience again as the exiles.

> What God is saying here to Zion's children - in the plural - is this: I didn't divorce your mother (when I sent Zion into exile), and the proof is that she can show no certificate....[131]

In sum, Knight views the terms "Zion" and "Jerusalem" as crucial metaphors in determining the audiences of Deutero-Isaiah. At times he recognizes the parallelism "Zion/Jerusalem" as a metaphor for the city, but "the city" is the people in exile! Zion can refer to the exiles as the beloved wife of Yahweh. When used with a plural form, Zion again means the exiles. But for Knight "Zion" also refers to the physical area around Judah, including small towns and villages.[132] Then regarding 51:16, Knight states that "Zion" can also denote the whole people Israel. Jerusalem, when used with the feminine singular form, refers to the city in exile, Yahweh's bride. Even when the words (Zion/Jerusalem) are not used, Knight argues that they

---

[127] Knight, 161.

[128] Knight, 161.

[129] Knight, 161.

[130] Knight, 95.

[131] Knight, 143.

[132] Knight, 15.

are implied by the singular/plural and feminine/masculine forms of "you" or "your" (see 45:14, p.95). Therefore, it would appear that Knight understands Deutero-Isaiah's audience as primarily the exiles and secondarily those left behind in Judah. For Knight, the Judahites are clearly included in the mind of Deutero-Isaiah. They are not to be ignored. Knight differs significantly from other commentators on Deutero-Isaiah in that he does not see the return to Jerusalem as the main theme (see Brueggemann, Hanson, Clifford). For Knight the center of Deutero-Isaiah's prophecies is "the revelation Deutero-Isaiah makes of the nature and purpose of God in His immanence in Israel as the Servant of the universe."[133] For this reason, Knight declares the work of Deutero-Isaiah as theology.

Jacob/Israel

Knight identifies the audience "Jacob/Israel" as primarily the exiles. He says the following in regards to 40:27.

> Israel in exile had supposed that Yahweh had forgotten her. The temple was lying in ruins, and the temple was that spot alone where God and man could meet in sacramental worship. Jerusalem was now destroyed, and Jerusalem alone was God's chosen city...The Holy Land, which God had given his people forever (Gen 17:8;28:13) was now overrun by hordes of heedless pagans...Their continued existence as a people even in far-off exile ought to show them that God has not repudiated his promise to Jacob.[134]

Knight argues that 41:14 supports the identity of "Jacob/Israel" as the exiles because he suspects that the use of the word "corpse" probably is a referral to death.

> But now he makes God say *you worm Jacob, you men of Israel*...But *you men of Israel* may be better rendered by *'you louse Israel'* thus putting *'louse'* in poetic parallel with *'worm'*.... The word *methey* in the Hebrew text has long been a puzzle...three important ancient versions translate it by a form of the word "dead"...By it he could be suggesting that Israel in exile has become a corpse, as Ezekiel had already done (37:11-13), so as that as a corpse Israel is also to be pictured in terms of worms and grubs.[135]

---

[133] Knight, 5.

[134] Knight, 23-24.

[135] Knight, 35.

Another image of "Jacob/Israel" as those in exile is that of a blind and deaf servant. In 43:22 God accuses "Jacob/Israel" of not calling on God or making sacrifices to Him while in exile.

> How tragic it is that for the fifty long years now that Israel has been in exile she has been blind to this underlying purpose of God... God had put her there to be his Servant in that particular situation, in fact, to be the means of offering to the gentiles the full life he wanted them to live. But now the eternal plan and purpose of God had failed. And it had failed through Israel's growing tired of God. [136]

Knight continues this line of argument highlighting the exiles' role as Servant while in exile.

> Since the exile had put an end to those daily and expensive offerings the opportunity had arisen for Israel to realize that she would now hold intimate communion with God without the instrumentality of the sacrificial cult...Yet, that glorious opportunity arising out of the discipline of the exiles, has been missed. [137]

In sum, the "Jacob/Israel" parallelism for Knight can be interpreted as the exiles in the majority of instances (e.g., 40:27; 41:8, 14; 43:22; 44:1). However, at times Knight uses phrases like "corporate entity" and "collective entity." According to Knight, these phrases are in line with the prophet's understanding of the covenant with Israel.

> For despite the fact that the Northern kingdom seemed to have been cut to pieces and its people scattered to the winds as much as a century and a half before the destruction of the Southern Kingdom, the prophets were certain that the reality of the covenant still held Israel together as one people in the sight of God...Thus Israel cannot finally perish: God's people are destined to return home where they belong - all of them, even those who are presently scattered to the ends of the earth. [138]

Like the earlier scholars cited, Knight supports a hint of inclusivity in chapters 40-55. Therefore, according to Knight, the exile was not a defeat for God, but rather the exiles were positioned in Babylonian exile to be a servant and because she failed to realize her purpose, she failed to be the

---

[136] Knight, 68.

[137] Knight, 69.

[138] Knight, 63-64.

people God called her to be.

Richard J. Clifford

Clifford dates chapters 40-55 sometime during the 540's and perhaps the 530's B.C.E. Clifford makes the following statement about the date and connects the date directly to the audience. He argues that "Deutero-Isaiah's words presuppose that Cyrus had already conquered Media (550 B.C.E.) and Lydia (547 B.C.E.). He entered Babylon in 539 B.C.E."[139] From the very outset, Clifford determines the primary audience as the exiles. Clifford states that "Chapters 40-55 are a collection of speeches of the 540's B.C.E. and perhaps the following decade, delivered to the Jews who had been deported to Babylon from their native Judah, a half century earlier..."[140] Clifford proceeds from the conclusion that Second Isaiah is "seventeen speeches of considerable length written in order to persuade his fellow Judahites in exile to leave Babylon and move towards Zion, the only place where they can become Israel."[141] He states that Deutero-Isaiah achieves his goal through the use of five polarities:

1) First and Last things
2) Babylon and Zion
3) Yahweh and the gods
4) Israel and the nations
5) The Servant and Israel. [142]

For Clifford, these five polarities are the key to the identity of the audiences. Unlike Westermann, Clifford does not view the genre as the primary clue to the formation of the text or the basic key to understanding who the audience is. He takes issue with the supporters of form criticism. In Clifford's opinion "the most damaging result of the over dominance of form criticism of Deutero-Isaiah is the determination of the length of units by considerations from genre rather than from the logic of the particular piece."[143]

---

[139] Richard J. Clifford, <u>Fair Spoken and Persuading: An Interpretation of Second Isaiah</u> (New York: Paulist, 1984), 9.

[140] Clifford, 3.

[141] Clifford, 5.

[142] Clifford, 5.

[143] Clifford, 34.

Therefore Clifford chooses to focus on the flow of the text and how the flow reveals a greater understanding of the author's message and the audience. He also points out how Deutero-Isaiah depends on structural parallelism (Israel, my servant, Jacob, whom I have chosen....) to persuade his audience. And on a larger scale, Second Isaiah makes use of the device of parallelism in opposing the Old Exodus-Conquest to the new act by which Israel comes into new existence. [144]

Clifford supports the position that the exiles are the primary audience and that Jerusalem is the only place where Israel can truly be the servant of God. For Clifford, "Zion is preeminently the place of divine disclosure, from Zion shall go forth the teaching, the word of Yahweh from Jerusalem." [145] Clifford uses even stronger language in his understanding of the pre-exilic prophetic scenario, which, he argues, explains Deutero-Isaiah's comparison of the Exile and the Exodus. Clifford states that once judgment has occurred, restoration follows. This requires the acquisition of the land after the Exodus, and a return to the land for the exiles. For presence in the land determines the identity of Israel as God's people. Therefore, "...Israel becomes truly Israel when it engages in the act of returning, when it leaves Babylon and crosses the desert to Zion."[146]

Included in Clifford's five polarities are several possible audiences. However, they all bring the reader back to the primary audience, the exiles.

Zion

Clifford views Zion as the term that "Second Isaiah favors for Jerusalem." [147] Clifford treats the parallelism as if the two words were one unit. We see evidence of this in 40:9.

---

[144] Clifford, 43.

[145] Clifford, 76.

[146] Clifford, 26.

[147] Clifford, 76.

> Go up to a high mountain, O Zion,
> Messenger of good tidings
> Raise your voice aloud, Jerusalem,
> Messenger of good tidings.

The structural parallelism here suggests that Zion and Jerusalem are a unit. Clifford states that this is part of the polarity that exists in Deutero-Isaiah to bring clarity about the coming downfall of Babylon. Therefore for Clifford, "the call to Zion to 'go up' is meant to contrast with the command to Babylon to 'go down' from her throne in Isa 47:1, Dame Babylon being the antithesis of Dame Zion in Second Isaiah."[148] Clifford goes into great detail to describe the significance of the "Zion" metaphor in Deutero-Isaiah. He argues that "Zion as the site of the Temple,...is the place where cosmic victory took place, where Yahweh's power is displayed and where the same power protects his people."[149] Although Clifford identifies "Zion" as the city, he does not recognize the Judahites as a significant audience in Deutero-Isaiah. Clifford acknowledges that much of the population of Judah was deported, implying that some remained.[150] Then he states later that "other nations moved in to occupy the land of Judah."[151] Therefore, it seems that for Clifford there was perhaps no major audience of Israelite people left in Judah. Nonetheless, the city is addressed, if only for its former and its future role.

Clifford finds Deutero-Isaiah's final reference to "Zion" in chapters 54 and 55. In Clifford's opinion, these two chapters center on "Zion", "the former emphasizing the security of the holy city now that its Husband and Creator has returned, and the later, the city's visibility to the nations as a center of life."[152]

The Exiles

Clifford argues that 40:1-11 focuses on the people of Judah and the coming activity there, the ultimate geographical goal of the exiles. Then Deutero-Isaiah turns to the exiles in his second speech, 40:12-31.

---

[148] Clifford, 76.

[149] Clifford, 127.

[150] Clifford, 3.

[151] Clifford, 80.

[152] Clifford, 184.

According to the previous section (40:1-11), Zion is the goal of the march homeward. The prophet now turns his attention to those at the other end of the road - the exiles in Babylon. These he must persuade that their national God, Yahweh, is aware of their exhaustion from captivity...and is able to strengthen them.[153]

Since Clifford dates chapters 40-55 sometime around the 540's it is obvious that for him Deutero-Isaiah is addressing the second or third generation of exiles. This being the case, Deutero-Isaiah has a difficult time persuading this audience to leave Babylon (for most the only home they have known), and go to Zion, an unwalled city in ruins. Westermann suggested that Deutero-Isaiah used code words that only the audience knew the true meaning of.[154] Clifford agrees that the message was indeed recognizable to those to whom it was addressed.

> He spoke....to a community that was alert and fully capable of appreciating his condense, argumentation and of considering his call to action.... He counts on the tradition to be so deeply ingrained in his audiences' heart and head that mere hints suffice for the whole to be called up. [155]

The language is meant to trigger loyalty in the audience and remind the exiles of their existence before the exile. Therefore, for Clifford, "Language of the choosing of individuals such as Jacob, Abraham, David, is applied to the choosing of the whole people." [156]

In what Clifford calls the 9th Speech (ch 46) we encounter the "remnant" language.

> Listen to me, O house of Jacob,
> all the remnant of the house of Israel..(46:3ab)

The "remnant" makes reference to the exiles, "suggesting that Israel as exiled is contrasted with Babylon as exiled."[157] This again is a part of the

---

[153] Clifford, 79.

[154] Westermann, 69.

[155] Clifford, 38.

[156] Clifford, 91.

[157] Clifford, 130.

"Zion/Babylon" polarity that Clifford proposes as a key to understanding Deutero-Isaiah and his audiences.

In agreement with Westermann, Clifford interprets the language as evidence supporting the exiles as the audience in chapter 46. This chapter not only features the audience as the exiles but also uses language noting the importance of a return to Zion. For Clifford, "Even more important, the verbs of carrying suggest that Yahweh will carry his people to a restored city of Zion." [158] Then in 46:8-11, we find the term *psy'm* "rebel." Clifford identifies the "rebels" as "those exiled Israelites who have refused to acknowledge that their God has carried them in the past and is about to carry them in the future."[159] Clifford continues this line of argument when interpreting 46:13 as evidence that the exiles are the intended audience.

> 'Far from my justice' is not a metaphor; it describes the actual physical state of the 'remnant of the house of Israel.' They are in Babylon, far from Zion where Yahweh has chosen to dwell and to speak his words that give order to the world, i.e. his "justice" and his "salvation".... The destruction of Babylon and the flight of its helpless gods send a clear message to Israel: do not keep yourselves from the shrine of God, Zion.[160]

In sum, it is obvious that the exiles are the primary audience for Clifford. Although he states that the return from exile is not the central theme of the chapters, he argues throughout his commentary that "Zion" is the only place where the exiles can receive their restoration and be witnesses to the whole world. Clifford argues that "the Zion-Babylon polarity makes clear that Zion is the only place where Yahweh can be worshiped. Babylon is the land of the tyrant and is full of false gods." [161]

Jacob/Israel

Clifford does not address the parallelism "Jacob/Israel" as a group. For him, the "Jacob/Israel" parallelism is included in the polarity "Israel and the Nations." He interprets all the passages that use this parallelism as addressed to those in exile. For Clifford, the "Jacob/Israel" parallelism in

---

[158] Clifford, 131.

[159] Clifford, 131.

[160] Clifford, 132.

[161] Clifford, 46.

the lament found in 40:27 is an example of how "the exiles assumed that Fate now favors the Babylonians who defeated and now rule them, and the other nations who moved in to occupy the land of Judah."[162] Clifford concludes that the audience here is the exiles.

The Nations/Coastlands

According to Clifford's classification of polarities, the nations as audience is a part of the polarity "Yahweh and the gods." In what Clifford calls the third speech (41:1-42:9), the nations are addressed in 41:1-7.[163] This is evidenced by the parallelism of coast lands and nations.

> Be silent before me coast lands,
> Let the nations wait for my decision
>
>   41:1

The nations have been called to assemble but the call has frightened them. Clifford states that "The nations draw near in fright, reassuring each other that the passive images they themselves have constructed will somehow save them from Yahweh's judgment."[164]

Clifford argues that although the nations are called to gather in the fifth speech (43:9-44:5) the harsh tone is meant for Israel.

> The present speech (not drama) focuses exclusively on Israel and adopts a rebuking tone for the most part. The scene of the assembly of the nations can be shaped differently for different purposes....the nations are summoned to a trial in which they are told to witness to their god's power, Israel being singled out as Yahweh's witnesses. [165]

Clifford points out that this is the first occurrence of the word "witness" in Deutero-Isaiah. Israel's role as witness is directly connected to the nations' call to gather. The role of witness was once the responsibility of the king only. Deutero-Isaiah reassigns that role to the people. Clifford makes this point in the sixth speech (44:6-23). For Clifford, "the role of witness to the patron deity's power, once done by the king as the divine agent, is now

---

[162] Clifford, 80.

[163] Clifford, 89.

[164] Clifford, 91.

[165] Clifford, 92.

fulfilled by the people."[166] Although Clifford recognizes the nations and coast lands as witnesses to the *mspt* of Israel's God, he does not view their role as major. Instead he says "the nations are part of important scenes as chorus, not as protagonist."[167]

Cyrus and Babylon

Cyrus. There are two additional audiences mentioned in Deutero-Isaiah -- Cyrus and Babylon. Cyrus is only addressed and mentioned by name in chapter 45 and, according to Clifford, the speech to Cyrus is related to the creation victory in fashioning order from chaos.[168]

> Ancient Near Eastern creation accounts tell how the god built his temple after conquering chaos and making the world habitable. The temple was the place where the victory was especially manifest, since the gods' heavenly glory was visible to people there. By his choosing Cyrus, Yahweh is declaring the Persian to be the instrument of his creation; hence he (Cyrus) is the appropriate builder of the Temple. [169]

Clifford argues that Cyrus's role is to take on the responsibilities of past kings in history. "The people are invited to believe in the power of God, becoming visible in the person of Cyrus. They are to watch his victory as the victory of their God, and allow Cyrus to send them home to celebrate in the rebuilt Temple."[170] The phrase, "send them home" supports the position that the exiles are the ultimate addressee, even though the name Cyrus is used.

Babylon. Babylon (ch 47) is only relevant for Clifford because it serves as a "counter image" of Zion, the Holy City. [171] Babylon has served her purpose, to punish Israel. Now, it is her turn to "sit in the dust."

---

[166] Clifford, 111.

[167] Clifford, 178.

[168] Clifford, 119.

[169] Clifford, 119.

[170] Clifford, 121.

[171] Clifford, 135.

The Servant

Clifford views the "servant" as a title or role. In ch 49 (the 12th speech), the word "servant" is used four times (vv 3, 5-7). The identity of the servant is tied into the vocation of the servant. It is the "servant's vocation in Second Isaiah to lead Israel to a new Exodus-Conquest. It is not surprising that his call is modeled on the commission of Moses in Exod 3:1-4:17..."[172] Clifford views the "servant" as a calling for Israel to respond to. This is one of the five polarities that Clifford uses to interpret Second Isaiah's message -- the Servant and the People.

> The "servant" is what all Israel is called to become...The servant is therefore Israel obedient to the divine word. The servant can of course be an individual but all Israel is called to obey the word through him, and the concept can include those Israelites who are associated with the servant in obedience to the present task.[173]

Yet as "servant" the people in exile are called to leave Babylon and return to Jerusalem.

> Because the servant in Second Isaiah is not a private individual who acts in isolation from people, his action affects the whole community intimately. The servant can stand for the people. The whole people is called to leave Babylon and to return to Jerusalem in a new Exodus-Conquest. Not all obeyed the summons. Not all realized the profound reasons why the Exile took place and consequently did not "offer their back to the smiter" (50:6), i.e. did not accept it as divine punishment. Not all were zealous for the glory of Yahweh; they did not allow themselves to be gathered as Israel so as to prove to the nations that Yahweh is a living God. Not all were willing to obey the command to return when it meant a dangerous journey home to claim property now held by others, to give up property certainly held, and a position in the Babylon community. The servant embraced all these tasks, and through him Israel came to life again.[174]

In sum, Clifford concludes that the exiles are the primary audience. He uses five polarities to identify the character of the audiences and their role in the plan of comfort.

Zion is the city, but there is no significant audience in Jerusalem.

---

[172] Clifford, 150.

[173] Clifford, 153.

[174] Clifford, 57-58.

Finally, the role of servant is a calling for Israel to respond to, for only as servant are the people called to leave Babylon and return to Jerusalem.

Paul Hanson

Hanson dates chapters 40-66 between 550-515 B.C.E. (He does not give a separate date for chapters 40-55).[175] In regards to the literary organization of the chapters, Hanson disagrees with what he sees as Westermann's insistence on labeling the genres of Deutero-Isaiah solely on the basis of the structure of earlier genres.

> ....attempts to analyze it by applying the templates of earlier genres, such as one finds in the important commentary of Claus Westermann, often end up being forced. The categories that may be helpful in studying Hosea and Amos do not always fit the material in these chapters.... The old wineskins no longer were adequate, abetting the productions of new containers.[176]

Hanson uses even stronger language against Westermann's categorical use of genre.

> If one pays more attention to the text than to the canons of a modern method of interpretation, a different understanding of Isaiah 48 commends itself. The words of accusation are carefully woven into the fabric of what proves to be a carefully nuanced message. Second Isaiah emerges as a much more subtle thinker than Westermann's form-critically correct prophet who is incapable of complex thought.[177]

However, this does not mean that Hanson is in total agreement with the rhetorical criticism perspective. For Hanson, "The other extreme, though, is correspondingly inappropriate. James Muilenburg...tears Second Isaiah from important roots when he describes a poet working with the complicated structures of a modern composer."[178]

Hanson, therefore, finds himself in a different category than his predecessors in his analysis of the literary composition of chapters 40-55.

---

[175] Paul D. Hanson, Isaiah 40-66, (John Knox Press: Louisville, 1995), 1.

[176] Hanson, 12.

[177] Hanson, 123.

[178] Hanson, 123.

He concludes that the literary organization is open to new interpretations and change.

> Second Isaiah the poet, like Second Isaiah the thinker, draws on the old to create the new. The resulting literary product cannot be reduced to stanzas and movements any more than it can be boxed in trials, disputations, promises, threats, and exhortations. This behooves us to remain attentive to ways in which the prophet draws on older genres as well as ways in which she or he reshapes them to address a rapidly changing world. [179]

Deutero-Isaiah's primary audience, for Hanson, is the exiles. Although he acknowledges the existence of those left behind in Judah, they are not a major focus for Deutero-Isaiah's message.

> The exiles, on balance, enjoyed better chances of prospering in commerce and trade than their kinsfolk who had remained on native soil. Whereas the Babylonians granted their captive guests considerable freedom to enter into business relationships, the people dwelling in Judah occupied a land that had been left in ruins both by the original Babylonian destruction and by successive waves of marauders, such as the Edomites who swept over crippled Judah in search of plunder." [180]

Hanson does not refer to the Judahite residents in any significant way in the remainder of his commentary.

The Exiles

From the very beginning of his commentary Hanson sets up the context and location of chapters 40-55.

> As a result of the devastating attack of the Babylonian armies earlier in that century, a large segment of the population of Judah now dwelled as captives and exiles along the banks of the Euphrates surrounded by worshipers of Marduk and Nebo and the other members of the Babylonian pantheon.[181]

Hanson also regards the exiles as the original audience.

Regarding the original audience, we must remember that many of the

---

[179] Hanson, 12.

[180] Hanson, 1

[181] Hanson, 1.

prophet's contemporaries were asking whether there was any source of comfort left for a people stripped of self-defense, vulnerable before their captors, bitter of soul as they mourned in a foreign land.[182]

For Hanson, the author of Deutero-Isaiah lived among the exiles. Hanson argues this position based on Deutero-Isaiah's observations of the cultic life around him and his continuous references to the captives' return home through the wilderness.

> Although it is disputed by some scholars, most assume that Second Isaiah crafted the message found in Isaiah 40-55 (as well as chaps. 34-35) while living with the exiles in Babylon. Vivid descriptions of Babylonian cultic practices as well as announcements of Yahweh's coming to return the captives over a wilderness route to their native land argue for this setting.[183]

Hanson employs several arguments to support his position that the exiles are the primary audience in Deutero-Isaiah. First, he argues that the use of creation language (40:12) is a strategy of Deutero-Isaiah to encourage those in exile to remain faithful to the God who not only created Israel, but also the universe.

> Opening the minds and hearts of the people to the possibility of deliverance from bondage begins with displaying the vastness of the universe as evidence of God's majesty and power. To contemplate the One who can weigh the mountains and measure the heavens is to lift the mind toward the One who alone is capable of returning a captive nation to its home.[184]

Secondly, because of their depressed state, Hanson argues that Deutero-Isaiah used the language of war to remind the exiles of what a mighty warrior God has been for them in the past. He states the following in regards to 42:10-17.

> As if to shake any lingering inertia out of the members of the community, the archaic image of God acting as Divine Warrior completes the hymnic introduction to this unit...Perhaps it helps to picture the rousing of the Divine Warrior as the reentry into society of awareness of the God who empowers the oppressed and who calls the family of nations to tender concern for nature and its delicate harmony.[185]

---

[182] Hanson, 14.

[183] Hanson, 2.

[184] Hanson, 28.

[185] Hanson, 49-50.

Thirdly, Hanson states that Deutero-Isaiah used polemic to disavow any belief that the Babylonian "idol gods" were stronger than Yahweh. The exiles were bombarded with images of "idols" who claimed to be superior to Israel's God.[186] Deutero-Isaiah addressed the problem creatively with the trial speech and the disputation. Hanson notes the following.

> The ubiquity of such polemic, however, illustrates the intensity of the threat posed by the gods of Babylon to the people living in exile. The Yahwistic confessions of Israel stood as an exception to the traditional beliefs of Mesopotamia. To rest the case for one's God on evidence from the ambiguous realm of history rather than on the eternal myth and ritual of temple priests and the exalted science of astrologers ran counter to the prevailing orthodoxy. Second Isaiah returned repeatedly to the issue of the idols because it represented a deadly threat to the spiritual existence of the exilic community. [187]

These three arguments provide for Hanson strong evidence in favor of the exiles as the primary audience in Deutero-Isaiah

Zion/Jerusalem

Hanson views the parallelism "Zion/Jerusalem" as one of the code phrases that refers to three things: a herald (40:9); the exiles (41:27); and the city (52:1-2).

"Zion/Jerusalem" as Herald (40:9)

In 40:9, Deutero-Isaiah addresses "Zion/Jerusalem" as the audience. Zion/Jerusalem" is told to proclaim the good news to all the land. Here "Zion/Jerusalem" is viewed as a herald, a proclaimer of news, a carrier of a message from God to those in Jerusalem, in the cities of Judah (which in terms of the former kingdom of Judah, could include the people in Benjamin), and in exile.

> "Zion/Jerusalem", the recipient of God's words of comfort in v 1, is here commissioned to proclaim a joyous announcement to the rest of the land... here a word that strikes terror into the hearts of the ungodly becomes for repentant Israel a word addressing Israel's dilemma in exile with the joyous proclamation that Israel had not been abandoned to the oppressor

---

[186] 2 Kings 18:19-35, the speech of Rabshakeh records the explicit claim to Assyrian superiority. God commands the Assyrian army to conquer therefore, God cannot counter the Assyrian army.
[187] Hanson, 113.

but was under the loving care of a God both great and good.[188]

Hanson continues to argue the role of "Zion/Jerusalem" as herald in a later section of his commentary. In his analysis of 40:9, Hanson states that, "... Zion/Jerusalem was personified as a 'herald of good tidings' with instructions to announce the arrival of God who both as victorious warrior and as gentle shepherd, brings deliverance to the exiled people."[189] As herald, "Zion/Jerusalem" addresses those in exile and proclaims a message of comfort. This message is to go forth from the city into all the surrounding areas. But the primary audience is those in exile. As God prepares the location for their return, the exiles must prepare to receive their God and leave Babylon.

"Zion/Jerusalem" as the Exiles (41:27)

Hanson interprets the "Zion/Jerusalem" parallelism in 41:27 as referring to the exiles.[190] In 41:27 Deutero-Isaiah uses the disputation to prove to the exiles that the gods of Babylonia are nothing, powerless, and unable to direct or predict the future. Their fear that Yahweh has somehow abandoned them and no longer has compassion for them is unwarranted. Yahweh is in charge of human history and their liberation is inevitable.

> Does the fact that God rules over the heavens and the earth remove from Israel the oppression of exile and the pains of servitude under the Babylonian empire? ...Therefore, the people could be confident that even in Babylon their Lord remains the force directing the events of human history to accomplish their liberation.[191]

"Zion/Jerusalem" as the City

Hanson argues that in 52:1-2 "Zion/Jerusalem" is portrayed as a "city in exile." He uses this imagery in concert with 51:17-23 where "Zion/Jerusalem" is not used as a parallelism. In 51:17-23, "Zion" and "Jerusalem" "both depict the Holy City as a mother of the children of

---

[188] Hanson, 24.

[189] Hanson, 133.

[190] Hanson, 34.

[191] Hanson, 34.

Israel."¹⁹² According to Hanson, the imagery was already in the mind of the audience for "the image used to describe the tragic loss Jerusalem has suffered is one that was widely used by the exilic community to portray God's judgment (Jer 5:15,17,28;49:12; Ezek. 23:33; Ps. 75:8; Lam. 4:21)."¹⁹³

Hanson finds additional support for the imagery of "Zion/Jerusalem" as a city in exile in the mythology of the ancient Near Eastern cultures.

> In the mythic pattern, the celebration of the Warrior's return to his city would have been the end of the drama. King and people would have been at rest in their own land. In returning to Zion, however, Yahweh is returning to a city still in exile! ....the people must march back to their homeland. ¹⁹⁴

Here Hanson not only supports the argument that the people must return to Jerusalem in order to fulfill their calling and be a witness, but throughout his commentary, Hanson focuses primarily on the exiles as the major audience of chapters 40-55. He finds reference to the exiles in every situation and context.

Jacob/Israel

Hanson rarely mentions the parallelism "Jacob/Israel." However, when interpreting the meaning of the "Jacob/Israel" parallelism, he simply refers to it as "Israel." Therefore, it appears that for Hanson the audience again is the exiles. Hanson first comments on the identity of "Jacob/Israel" in 41:9-11.

> Chapter 41:9-11 are personal and intimate. The God who has been praised as creator of the universe and the determiner of all destinies now draws near to assure the exiled people that they are embraced in tender love. The enduring quality of the relationship is highlighted by reference to Israel's ancestors, Jacob/Israel and Abraham. The words used to describe that historical relationship gives fullness to the picture of a covenant of steadfast love that endures even through crisis and adversity: "my servant", "whom I have chosen", "my friend."¹⁹⁵

---

¹⁹² Hanson, 147.

¹⁹³ Hanson, 148.

¹⁹⁴ Hanson, 150.

¹⁹⁵ Hanson, 38.

In subsequent appearances of the parallelism "Jacob/Israel," Hanson identifies the audience as the exiles (43:1, 22; 46:3) or implies that they are the audience based on the genre used--trial speech, disputation (42:4; 44:23; 45:4).

In sum, Hanson assumes that the parallelism "Jacob/Israel" is a reference to the exiles. He views the parallelism as a personal form of address that is used both in accusation and in assurance.[196]

Nations/Coast lands

The final possible audience for Hanson is the Nations/Coast lands.

> Be silent before me, you islands,
> Let the nations renew their strength
> Let them come forward and speak;
> Let us meet together as the place of judgment. 41:1

In Hanson's mind, the nations/coast lands are an avenue to inclusivity. Hanson argues that the gods of the nations have failed and now Israel's God must assert power over chaos.

> Because the patron gods of the nations have failed to uphold justice and thereby threaten the universe with the spector of a return to primordial chaos (all the foundations of the earth are shaken, Ps. 82:5) God asserts his power as defender of *mispat*, condemns the unjust gods, and assumes universal rule.[197]

This being the case, the exiles must now extend an invitation to the nations as Servant Israel.

> In contrast, ch 49 opens with a command to foreign peoples to listen and then describes Servant Israel as one bearing a commission that extends beyond domestic affairs to the welfare of the nations. But Israel's responsibilities extend beyond its borders to reach out to the nations of the earth.[198]

Hanson disagrees with anyone who "attempts to minimize or deny the universal dimension to Second Isaiah's concept of God's *mišpat*." To do so

---

[196] Hanson, 81.

[197] Hanson, 43.

[198] Hanson, 126.

is to "display ignorance of the fact that by nature the biblical concept of divine justice bears universal connotations (cf. 42:1, "justice to the nations," and 42:4, "justice in the earth and the coastlands")."[199]

For Hanson it becomes clear that the exiles are not only the primary audience in chapters 40-55, but they have a major role to play as witnesses to what God has already done and as the servant, whose task is to bring *mispat* into the world.

Walter Brueggemann

Brueggemann dates Deutero-Isaiah around 540 B.C.E.[200] Brueggemann is very clear about his position on the major audience in chapters 40-55. In Brueggemann's opinion, the primary theme of Deutero-Isaiah is "that Yahweh has defeated Babylon and Judah is free to depart exile..."[201] This theme is reiterated throughout the genres found in Deutero-Isaiah. Therefore Brueggemann agrees with some of the other scholars in viewing the literary genres as important clues to the message and audience of Deutero-Isaiah. Brueggemann focuses on the two major genres - the oracle of salvation and the speech of disputation - as evidence that the main audience of Deutero-Isaiah is the exiles.

> These twin modes of speech of disputation and oracle of salvation are quite distinct and move in opposite directions. But they need to be seen in relation to each other, for together they permit the exilic community to "see Yahweh"... The speech of disputation concerns the external world of the empire that threatens exilic Israel, whereas the oracle of salvation focuses upon the internal life of Israel...Taken together, the two rhetorical practices situate the majesty and mercy of Yahweh in the midst of exilic Israel.[202]

Brueggemann does not see the theme of Deutero-Isaiah as a complex one. Since Brueggemann focuses primarily on the exiles, he concludes that there are only three main characters.

> The primary story of these chapters is not very complex.... The dramatic

---

[199] Hanson, 43.

[200] Walter Brueggemann, Isaiah 40-66 (Louisville: Westminster John Knox Press, 1998), 3, 8.

[201] Brueggemann, 11.

[202] Brueggemann, 29.

depiction of Judah's life in exile....is concerned primarily with three characters: (1) Babylon...; (2) Judah, whether the reference is to the community of Israelites or Zion the city presented as being in exile, is the helpless victim of Babylon; (3) the unequal and exploitative relation between Babylon and Judah is beyond challenge until the arrival of a third party into the crisis namely, Yahweh....[203]

Yet, even though Brueggemann acknowledges three main characters, he still argues that there is one major audience - the exiles. He interprets the words and images in chapters 40-55 as describing the exiles and Deutero-Isaiah's attempt to persuade them to trust in the God of their ancestors. He gives very little attention to those remaining in the land for in his opinion, "what remains after the Babylonian incursion of 598 and the Babylonian devastation of 587 is a city in ruins, plus a scattering of Jews deported here and there."[204] Brueggemann also stresses the importance of a return to Jerusalem. This can be seen in his statements about the identity of those addressed in the text.

Judah

Brueggemann's first mention of Judah is found in his comments on 49:19-21. Here he suggests that the city of Jerusalem is uninhabited because of judgment.

> The ultimate image of judgment and ruin is that the city should be uninhabited, so that it becomes either a place for thorns and briers or a place of wild, unclean animals. It is the language of desolation that characterizes Jerusalem while the exiles are absent. Now, in an abrupt rhetorical reversal, the city will be repeopled with the exiles from Babylon.[205]

The image of an emptied city continues in 49:22-26. Those who were scattered throughout the world will be called out of their foreign places.

> But now, Yahweh will give a signal. Yahweh will motion to the nations. It is as though all powers in the earth keep their eye on Yahweh.... The nations know and respond. They know Yahweh is the commander, and they know Jews are treasured by Yahweh and belong in Jerusalem. The great homecoming to the heretofore emptied city is supreme evidence of

---

[203] Brueggemann, 11.

[204] Brueggemann, 8.

[205] Brueggemann, 117.

Yahweh's full sovereignty. Everyone can see it-Jews and Gentiles. [206]

From these statements one could assume that there are no people--or no people of any significance--in the land of Judah. But Brueggemann's comments later, in regards to 52:7-10, seem to suggest that their were some inhabitants left back in Judah. These verses offer a scenario of Yahweh's triumph in which there are four roles:

1) The "messenger" is the one who runs with exuberance all the way from Babylon to Jerusalem in order to carry "the good news" that Yahweh has decisively defeated the powers of Babylon...

2) The scenario includes the notion that *sentinels* are on the walls of ruined Jerusalem, partly to protect but primarily to await messengers from afar...Then they start shouting the news to the waiting inhabitants of ruined Jerusalem... They shout to the waiting populace.

3) The *ruins of Jerusalem* hear the report of the sentinels.... The *ruins of Jerusalem* may be understood as the defeated, dependent people of the city who had given up all expectation of well-being. Or the phrasing may refer to the actual stones and ruined walls and buildings left since 587 in scattered disarray like a typical war-torn city.

4) ....The reason the city rejoices...is because of Yahweh. [207]

Although Brueggemann recognizes the tradition that the land was totally destroyed and left empty, he does not ignore the texts of Deutero-Isaiah that suggest there were some people living in the land. However, he does not view the Judahites remaining in the land as a significant audience of concern in chapters 40-55.

Jacob/Israel

Brueggemann argues that the parallel "Jacob/Israel" is a code name for the people of Judah in exile. He states this in reference to 40:27-31.

---

[206] Brueggemann, 118.

[207] Brueggemann, 138-39.

For the first time in this extended doxological unit, the people of Judah are mentioned. The climax of this lyric concerns "Jacob, Israel". Creation faith comes down to the crisis of God's people in exile. The statement of verse 27 is a question. The poet apparently reiterates a complaint Judah voiced in exile, perhaps a complaint given stylized, liturgical expression. [208]

The parallelism refers to those in exile. In Brueggemann's opinion, Deutero-Isaiah focuses almost entirely on the exiles in Babylon. In addition, he refers to the prophet of chapters 40-55 as "Isaiah in exile."

> The intent of Second Isaiah is to reconstrue the life and history and destiny of exilic Israel by placing Yahweh at the center of its existence and discernment. Babylonian ideology had eliminated Yahweh from the horizon of Israel's historical possibility, and now the poet counters the effectiveness and persuasiveness of Babylonian propaganda. That is, the poet sets forth the gospel claim "See your God!" (40:9). [209]

> ...the primary rhetorical agenda of Isaiah in exile is to persuade exiles of Yahweh's power and reliability. [210]

Brueggemann is consistent in his interpretation of the parallelism "Jacob/Israel." In 41:8, where it is paralleled with Abraham and Sarah, Brueggemann states that the parallelism points to Deutero-Isaiah's preoccupation with the exilic community.

> ...in v.8, the poetry shifts into a new genre that is now completely preoccupied with the exilic community.... The address is full and reassuring, mobilizing the entire past through which Yahweh has established a peculiar relation with Israel. Connection is made to the ancestral, promissory stories of Genesis, with reference to both Jacob and Abraham... That is, the entire memory of Israel is mobilized in this moment in order to assure the exiles that this guaranteed relationship still operates and is decisive for the present and for the future. [211]

Deutero-Isaiah addresses the exiles in chapter 43 by using creation language as an apposition to the parallelism "Jacob/Israel." Brueggemann argues that Deutero-Isaiah tries to assure the exiles of their place in Yahweh's plan and

---

[208] Brueggemann, 26-27.

[209] Brueggemann, 28.

[210] Brueggemann, 68.

[211] Brueggemann, 33.

states that "Yahweh is deeply devoted to Israel and will act to liberate Israel from exile."[212] Brueggemann states that one of the goals of chapter 43 is to encourage the exiles and dispel any sense of abandonment.

> Now, in this present hour, Israel in exile is made freshly aware of Yahweh's profound commitment to Israel, a commitment that persists through and is undisturbed by any circumstance. The oracle is sounded around the double "Do not fear" of vv 1 and 5, an assurance designed to overcome Israel's exilic sense of abandonment.[213]

Brueggemann argues that "it is a recurring sense of Israel in exile that Yahweh has forgotten Israel and Yahweh's own covenant obligations to Israel..."[214] So in 44:21, Deutero-Isaiah tries to assure Israel that "Yahweh persists in care and attentiveness for Israel... Israel is a creature bound to Yahweh, and the product of Yahweh's generative work, and is not abandoned."[215] Brueggemann continues to interpret the "Jacob/Israel" parallelism as referring exclusively to the exiles (45:6; 46:3-4; 48:1, 12; 49:5-6).

Zion/Jerusalem

The parallelism "Zion/Jerusalem" occurs four times (40: 9; 41:27; 52:1, 2) in Deutero-Isaiah (Zion/Israel is found in 46:13). The term "Zion" occurs alone six times (49:14; 51:3, 11, 16; 52:7, 8) and the term "Jerusalem" occurs alone three times (40:2; 51:17; 52:9). For Brueggemann, whenever the parallelism appears, "Zion/Jerusalem" refers to the exiles. However, Brueggemann says the following in regards to the parallelism "Zion/Israel" found in 46:13.

> The double sense of of "salvation" is a promise and assurance that Israel's life - so long skewed by Babylon - is about to be made whole. The promise is to Zion, now about to be resettled in Jerusalem. Thus the final verse sounds the ultimate aim of this portion of Isaiah, the reconstitution of Judaism among the "survivors" of exile.[216]

---

[212] Brueggemann, 52.

[213] Brueggemann, 52.

[214] Brueggemann, 71.

[215] Brueggemann, 71.

[216] Brueggemann, 91.

Here Brueggemann explains how Deutero-Isaiah assigns the restoration of Israel to those in exile (Zion). Although Israel is "stubborn" and "far from righteousness," God promises to provide deliverance through Cyrus to those in Babylon and in turn Israel will receive the salvation of God's word.[217]

Jerusalem

In his introduction Brueggemann connects the term "Jerusalem" to those in exile. It is Jerusalem that is under judgment and that draws the negating attention of Yahweh (3:1, 8). It is Jerusalem that is addressed in exile - in recognition of its need and in assurance commensurate with its need (40:2; 44:28).

> It is Jerusalem that is imagined healed, restored, ransomed, forgiven (65:18-19). It is Jerusalem, the meeting place of divine will and historical reality that is the recipient of Yahweh's judgment and Yahweh's renewing comfort and mercy.[218]

For Brueggemann, 51:17-21, Jerusalem is called upon to "Rouse yourself, rouse yourself!", a call that "characterizes the miserable condition of Israel in exile".[219]

> The imperatives addressed to Yahweh in verse 9 are now addressed in turn to Jerusalem....Jerusalem is summoned to be alert, for something is about to happen that will matter enormously to Zion.... Verses 17b-21 characterize the miserable condition of Israel in exile. In substance, this is a *complaint* describing the situation of exile; however, it is spoken to Israel and not by Israel.[220]

Although "Jerusalem" is addressed, in Brueggemann's opinion the message is meant for Zion, the exiles! Therefore, the exiles remain the primary focus and audience.

---

[217] Brueggemann, 91.

[218] Brueggemann, 2.

[219] Brueggemann, 133.

[220] Brueggemann, 132.

Zion

When the term "Zion" is used outside of the parallelism, it refers both to the city (51:3, 11) and to the exiles (51:16). Yet, even when it refers to the city, Brueggemann takes it as referring to Zion in exile and again the exiles are the intended audience.

Brueggemann argues that the restoration and comfort of Zion, the city, is good news to the exiles. For they remember the earlier tradition that emphasized the destruction of Jerusalem. Now the exiles are told of a reversal. According to Brueggemann, "The utterance in imperative and assurance defies present exilic circumstance and looks to renewal assured by Yahweh, who is now again the dominant force in Israel's life."[221]

Nations/Coast lands

Although it appears that the "nations/coast lands" are being addressed, for Brueggemann it is the exiles who hear the message. This is probably the case when Deutero-Isaiah uses the trial scene and the disputations concerning the gods of Babylon.

> The purpose of the poetry is to communicate to the exiles how absurd it is to trust or fear or obey Babylonian gods. The exiles are invited to count on Cyrus and to anticipate a new historical possibility, precisely because they count upon Yahweh. The large claim is that although Babylon appears to control history, the real ruler is Yahweh.[222]

Brueggemann continues this argument in his analysis of 41:1-2. He states that "This speech of disputation conducts an imagined courtroom trial in which listening exilic Israel observes while the claims of rival gods are adjudicated." [223]

Then, in 48:14, Brueggemann interprets the phrase, "Assemble, all of you, and hear!" addressed to Israel. However, he does not rule out the possibility that it may be addressed to the nations or their gods.[224] Nevertheless, the real audience is the exiles. Brueggemann concludes that "The exiles are here led to identify, trust, and heed the true Dispatcher of

---

[221] Brueggemann, 126.

[222] Brueggemann, 32.

[223] Brueggemann, 30.

[224] Brueggemann, 105.

imperial history."[225]

Deutero-Isaiah's final mention of "coast lands" is found in 49:1. Here Brueggemann detects a note of inclusivity. He is open to the possibility that a new audience is introduced here.

> The servant speaks to announce his mandate from Yahweh. The address to "coast lands and peoples" is ambiguous. (See the same word pair in 41:1) It may be that this is a global invitation to all peoples. Conversely, it may be that it is an address to Jews who have been scattered in the Diaspora in the wake of the destruction of Jerusalem. In either case, the servant is to be recognized in a very large vista, with a sweeping mandate and a large ambition.[226]

Brueggemann includes all exiles from 'the ends of the earth' in these comments. But wherever exile exists, there is a need for a herald to proclaim a message of comfort.

Sub-groups in the Exile

In Deutero-Isaiah there appears to be sub-groups among the exiles who are addressed. In 50:4, Brueggemann accuses one sub-group of attacking the servant.

> It seems more likely to me that the abuse comes from other members of the exilic community who have worked out a sustainable compromise between Yahweh and the empire, who do not want to have the compromise exposed or questioned and who do not want to be pressed to decide for Yahweh and for the disruptive venture of homecoming in a distinctive identity.[227]

Brueggemann identifies a sub-group in 51:1 that may function as an inner circle. He identifies a "summons to Israel" that is addressed to "the pursuers of righteousness" and "the seekers of Yahweh," that is, the ones deeply serious about faith.[228] For Brueggemann, Deutero-Isaiah continues to suggest the possibility of rival groups within the camp of the Babylonian exiles. In looking at 51:7, there seems to be evidence of rival sub-groups who were not in support of Deutero-Isaiah's vision. Brueggemann states the following.

---

[225] Brueggemann, 106.

[226] Brueggemann, 110.

[227] Brueggemann, 122.

[228] Brueggemann, 125.

The reference is not clear; it may be to the Babylonians who mock Israel's peculiar identity, or it is possible that the reproach and revilement reflect internal disputes in the community of Jewish exiles between those who accommodate to Babylonian insistence and those who resist any accommodations on the grounds of faith. It is most likely that this assurance is for the zealous in the community of exiles "who have my teaching in their hearts." [229]

In sum, it appears that Brueggemann believes that Deutero-Isaiah is focused on one audience in particular--the exiles. Brueggemann admits that Deutero-Isaiah uses creative language to get his points across, but, for Brueggemann, it always returns to the exiles as the primary audience. The exiles are divided in their receptivity towards Deutero-Isaiah's message of comfort, which often time causes Deutero-Isaiah to remind them of their history with God, of their exemplary ancestors (Noah, Abraham, Sarah and David), and of their special status as God's own creation. It is part of Deutero-Isaiah's strategy to remind the people in exile of God's power and sovereignty, as well as to convince the exiles that the gods of Babylonia are nothing. Those in Judah play a minor role in what is about to happen, but for Brueggemann, it must happen in Jerusalem, and not in Babylonia.

Karl Baltzer

Klaus Baltzer dates chapters 40-55 later than most scholars. He allows that it could be no later than "the end of the sixth century," but he favors a final date sometime between 450 and 400 B.C.E., which identifies the Servant as Nehemiah. [230] Baltzer views chapters 40-55 as a liturgical drama that was composed in Jerusalem.[231] He argues that it was performed for the *gola* during the spring festival Passover/Mazzot. [232] The audience is "Israelites and sympathizers..."[233]

Baltzer divides chapters 40-55 into six acts, "framed by a prologue and an epilogue."[234] Within these six acts, Baltzer recognizes the many

---

[229] Brueggemann, 128.

[230] Klaus Baltzer, <u>Deutero-Isaiah</u> (Minneapolis:Fortress Press, 2001), 30.

[231] Baltzer, 24.

[232] Baltzer, 22.

[233] Baltzer, 24.

[234] Baltzer, 15.

arguments put forward by Deutero-Isaiah in order to get the audiences to change their opinions and behavior.

For Baltzer, divine speech predominates.[235] Baltzer argues that what is new for Deutero-Isaiah "is the close bond between the renewal of Jacob/Israel and the renewal of Zion/Jerusalem."[236] For Baltzer, these two parallelisms are the center of Deutero-Isaiah's message. His analysis of the parallelisms is both unique and creative. Together, the parallelisms represent both male (Jacob/Israel) and female (Zion/Jerusalem). Baltzer argues that for Deutero-Isaiah that portrays the whole people.[237]

Jacob/Israel

Baltzer also acknowledges that the two parallelisms "Jacob/Israel" and "Zion/Jerusalem" "are given equal space and equal attention in Deutero-Isaiah's account. In both, the political and religious aspects play a part. In both city and countryside there are rich and poor (49:24-26)."[238] It appears that for Baltzer, "Jacob/Israel" represents the countryside (the cities of Judah). This characterization of "Jacob/Israel" is not found in the other scholars who have been reviewed. Baltzer assumes a political connection between Jerusalem and the cities of Judah (40:9-11, 44:26). This political connection dictates a differentiated society. The intellectuals live in the city and the shepherds and farmers reside in the countryside (44:14-20).[239] Therefore, for Balzer, there are three basic classifications of audience: the city (Zion/Jerusalem), the country (Jacob/Israel), and the Diaspora.[240] He states that "Deutero-Isaiah's program is to link city, country, and Diaspora. The people belonging to these different sectors constitute the new Israel as the people of God."[241]

Using the double name "Jacob/Israel" presents a possible problem for interpretation. Baltzer argues that for Deutero-Isaiah "It may perhaps be a

---

[235] Baltzer, 6.

[236] Baltzer, 30.

[237] Baltzer, 82.

[238] Baltzer, 32.

[239] Baltzer, 32.

[240] Baltzer, 32.

[241] Baltzer, 32.

way of showing the plurality and the unity."[242] Throughout chapters 40-55, Deutero-Isaiah goes back and forth between the singular and plural forms when referring to "Jacob/Israel." The parallelism is accompanied by several appositions that describe "Jacob/Israel" as "my servant" (41:8), "called" (43:22) or "formed" (43:1). Baltzer argues that in the role as "servant" "Jacob/Israel" functions as the personification of God's people.[243]

Regarding 46:3, Baltzer views the parallelism as probably a reference to the Babylonian gola.[244] He bases this conclusion on the phrase, "the whole remnant of the house of Israel."

> The remnant of a people actually served originallyl as a witness to its complete downfall in judgment and war. It was a long time before the remnant idea could be interpreted positively, as a sign of the compassion of Israel's God. It was probably only in the postexilic period that it became a sustaining theologoumenon with which to acknowledge new salvation after the catastrophe.[245]

Then again in 49:6, wherein he sees the Servant perhaps identified with Moses, Baltzer identifies the parallelism "Jacob/Israel" as the exiles, perhaps in two senses: "This can mean the people who were left over at the exodus, but it is also a transparent reference to the return of the exiles, which was Dt Isa's (Deutero-Isaiah's) contemporary situation." [246]

Baltzer sums up the purpose of the "Jacob/Israel" parallelism in 44:3-5. Here Baltzer argues that Deutero-Isaiah's focus is on the revival of the people in exile and the return to Jerusalem.

> Attention has been drawn - rightly I believe - to the closeness between this passage and Ezek 37:1-4, the vision of the "raising of dead Israel." There the Spirit brings the "dry bones" to life again. The subject is the revivification of the people and the return to the land.... I believe DtIsa's initial point is the restoration of God's people.... If Jacob is a servant, his descendants are servants too, and the gift of the Spirit is given to them...[247]

---

[242] Baltzer, 82.

[243] Baltzer, 96.

[244] Baltzer, 258.

[245] Baltzer, 258.

[246] Baltzer, 310.

[247] Baltzer, 186-87.

Zion/Jerusalem

The parallelism "Zion/Jerusalem" is a compound for Baltzer that "embraces the city as a whole." He argues the following.

> Although the two names also become largely congruent with one another ("Zion" standing for the whole of Jerusalem and "Jerusalem" for the city chosen by Yahweh), the name "Jerusalem" nevertheless stresses the political stature of the city more emphatically. It is the more comprehensive term. When the two terms appear together in compound form, fused into a single personification, this no doubt embraces the city as a whole, as a religious and political entity and brings out the unity of the two aspects.[248]

The "Zion/Jerusalem" parallelism is usually expressed with the aid of female personification. This runs throughout chapters 40-55. In 40:9, "Zion/Jerusalem" is acting as one who passes on a piece of news...Zion/Jerusalem has to be seen as a (female) messenger."[249] Baltzer states that the "Zion" in the parallelism is "topographically the name of Jerusalem's eastern hill... the name acquires a preeminently religious connotation as the place of Yahweh's presence, which is associated with the temple. Yahweh has chosen Zion. That is his dwelling place and the place of his throne...."[250]

Baltzer argues that after 49:14 the "Zion/Jerusalem" parallelism is the main figure. He states that this probably suggests that there were different groups with different audiences.

> In this way DtIsa (Deutero-Isaiah) links two concepts with differing traditions - the idea of God's people as Jacob/Israel, and the idea of God's city as Zion/Jerusalem. It seems probable that the two themes were fostered by different groups and that they had different addressees. But both themes are already programmatically stated in the prologue to chap. 40 (see 40:1 and 2; cf. 51:16).[251]

Baltzer declares that the tensions are between the concept of "Zion/Jerusalem" as a real city and its inhabitants and the personification of

---

[248] Baltzer, 62.

[249] Baltzer, 61.

[250] Baltzer, 62.

[251] Baltzer, 319.

the parallelism. This is because the imagery implies the rise of "Zion/Jerusalem" over against the fall of Babylon.[252]

Baltzer argues that "Zion" represents different groups in chapters 40-55. In 49:14-21 Baltzer states that there are three different variations on the theme of "Zion": 1) Zion can be a "woman who has not been forgotten" (49:14-16); 2) Zion will again look "like the bride" (49:17-19); and 3) Zion the "childless one who will have children" (v 20). In 49:14-50:1 the "Zion" imagery is viewed as woman, bride, and mother.[253]

Baltzer supports the argument that Jerusalem is the goal of the pilgrimage. He states that "Zion/Jerusalem is the city into which Yahweh enters as King (52:7) - i.e. it is 'the city of God.' This gives it a function as the goal of pilgrimage..."[254] He states further that "It is from the center in Zion/Jerusalem that the message is sent out."[255] For Baltzer, Deutero-Isaiah's goal is to connect the city to its people thereby determining who the people of God are.

Baltzer finds the relationship between the city of Jerusalem and the "cities of Judah" similar to the mother/child relationship.

> Childlessness and widowhood are the double fate that Jerusalem itself experienced (54:1,4)... As a woman, Jerusalem has in Yahweh lost her husband. The lost sons are the inhabitants of the city. But if the city is a "mother city," as in Greek... then her "children" are also the smaller cities that are subordinate to her...Yahweh is again Lord....Jerusalem's "widowhood" and "childlessness" are now at an end.[256]

"Zion/Jerusalem" is the place to which all must return. "Zion" is the goal of longing and hope. Zion is the place where God is present and people can live together in justice and peace."[257] She is the "spouse" of Yahweh. Her glorification represents the exaltation and return of Yahweh, her Husband. Israel in exile and in Diaspora is called back home. In 55:1-5, "she is

---

[252] Baltzer, 319.

[253] Baltzer, 321.

[254] Baltzer, 32.

[255] Baltzer, 62.

[256] Baltzer, 53.

[257] Baltzer, 319.

thereby inviting the people to make a pilgrimage to Jerusalem."[258]

The Nations/Coast lands

The "nations/coast lands" are a minor audience in Deutero-Isaiah. Baltzer identifies the "islands" (42:10) as the Greek world and the "nations" "are the nations of the territories from Egypt to Persia."[259] They have no role other than being "witnesses to an event rather than one of the parties in the proceedings."[260] He connects the role of the "nations/islands" to the conquest of Cyrus in 545 B.C.E.

> But because it is an exacting text, we may infer that if the islands and nations represent the Greek speaking countries along the Mediterranean coasts of Asia Minor, then they are mentioned as being the first countries that Cyrus subdued (c.545 B.C.E.). It was the winter war against Croesus of Lydia for the conquest of Sardis that first brought Cyrus renown. Now those who were vanquished witness to the cause of their defeat.[261]

For Baltzer the message is told to the "nations and islands" in order to assert Yahweh's claim that His sovereignty reaches to the ends of the earth."[262]

In sum, Baltzer views the parallelisms "Jacob/Israel" and "Zion/Jerusalem" as male and female counter parts representative of the

---

[258] Baltzer, 468.

[259] Baltzer, 26.

[260] Baltzer, 88.

[261] Baltzer, 89.

[262] Baltzer, 306.

whole nation. The drama is written in Jerusalem for an audience composed of the "Israelites and sympathizers." For this drama Baltzer establishes three classifications of audience: the city, the countryside and the Diaspora. "Jacob/Israel" becomes the personification of God's people in the role of servant. Baltzer also argues that the "Jacob/Israel" parallelism probably is, in addition, a reference to the Babylonian gola. The exiles must make the transfer to Jerusalem where they link up with city and country to become the new Israel.

Robert R. Wilson

As stated earlier, it is a thesis of this dissertation that the exiles are the primary audience of Deutero-Isaiah. Robert R. Wilson supports this argument by attempting to determine the community of Deutero-Isaiah. Wilson's strategy is first to examine the evidence at the beginning and the end of the exile through analysis of the political and religious situations.[263] Then Wilson compares the similarities and determines if any continuity exists between the two periods. From there Wilson attempts to determine the identity and characteristics of the community of Deutero-Isaiah and its profile during the exile.

Wilson bases his position on two familiar passages: 40:1-2 and 52:13-53:12. Wilson's audience is the exiles in general, but more specifically, the community of Deutero-Isaiah. In his opinion "God is speaking to only a part of Israel, and it makes sense to assume that God is addressing the disciples of Deutero-Isaiah, the group that treasured these oracles and saw itself playing an important role in realizing the prophecies that the book contains."[264]

In his comparison of the two periods (the beginning and the end of exile), Wilson developed a list of similarities: 1) there was a general acceptance of the Deuteronomistic explanation for why the exile happened; 2) permissible assimilation was discussed; 3) there was a possibility of a return to the land; 4) it was yet to be determined as to what the nature of the reconstructed state would be; 5) there were questions in regards to the nature and identity of the true Israel.[265] This evidence suggested for Wilson

---

[263] Robert R. Wilson, "The Community of Second Isaiah", Reading and Preaching the The Book of Isaiah. ed. C.R. Seitz (Minneapolis: Fortress, 1988), 54.

[264] Wilson, 54.

[265] Wilson, 61.

that "the late exilic period, the period of Deutero-Isaiah, was a period of political and religious controversy over the appropriate structure for a religious community in exile." [266]

Wilson argues that the community of Deutero-Isaiah was not widely accepted among the other exiles because of their unpopular political and religious positions. First, this group claimed that Cyrus was God's anointed ruler.[267] This claim, of course, rejected the Davidic line. Secondly, the community of Deutero-Isaiah considered itself "an elite group which God had set apart from the rest of the exiles for a particular task."[268] Thirdly, the group had strong links with the priestly tradition found in the Pentateuch.[269] Finally, the community of Deutero-Isaiah saw itself as God's servant and as a "newly purified community" who now must leave Babylon and return to the land.[270]

Wilson also states that the message must come from Jerusalem, not from Babylon.[271]

He offers the following striking rationale:

> The same principle could be applied to the sufferings of Zion itself. To be sure, Zion had originally sinned and had been punished through deserved destruction and exile...The group could now understand this undeserved measure of suffering, this unexpectedly long exile, not as a failure of God's justice but as a redemptive act on the part of the servant city. The city had suffered for the sake of the people, and that suffering would end in the restoration of the city to its former status as Yahweh's own chosen city, from which the divine redemptive word would go forth to all nations (40:9-11; 52:1-10). [272]

As God's servants, the community of Deutero-Isaiah envisioned "a transformation of Jerusalem into a priestly city from which the Torah of

---

[266] Wilson, 61.

[267] Wilson, 61.

[268] Wilson, 63.

[269] Wilson, 64.

[270] Wilson, 65.

[271] Wilson, 68.

[272] Wilson, 68.

Yahweh could go forth to the rest of Israel and ultimately the world."[273] Therefore, for Wilson, those exiles known as the community of Deutero-Isaiah are the audience and their role as servant is activated after the return to the city of Zion.

Robert Carroll

Most of the scholars presented in this chapter agree that the exiles are the major audience in Deutero-Isaiah. The second theme undergirding this chapter states that those left in Judah were a minor or insignificant audience.

Although some scholars agree that this group is addressed on some level, the controversy over the presence or absence of people in Jerusalem continues to stir the curiosity of scholars and provoke explanations that try to account for what happened to those left in the land. Most of these scholars wrote prior to E. Stern's analysis of archaeological evidence opposing any significant population in Jerusalem, though traditional Benjamin is a different matter.

Robert P. Carroll offers two reasons why the audience in Jerusalem--and he assumes there was such an audience--is not heard from or even considered important to the re-telling of the history of Israel during the exile and after the return. The first reason is found in the texts of 2 Kgs 25 and the 2 Chr 36:21. Both imply that there were no people of any importance left in the land. They were taken off to Babylonian exile or fled to Egypt (2 Kgs 25:26; Jer 40-41). Secondly, these texts support what is known as the "myth of the empty land," a land which for him--contrary to the archaeological evidence for Judah--was not at all empty. How this "myth" functions as a strategy of exclusion is argued by Carroll.

In his argument, Carroll describes the "myth of the empty land," "as an ideological story controlling membership in the new community."[274] It is this "myth" that allows the land to be empty in order to regain its holiness. Carroll argues that "the myth of the empty land holds the sacred enclave for the returnees, while allowing the land to regain its holiness after the period of pollution (2 Chr 36:14)."[275]

In Carroll's opinion the texts are used to substitute for political

---

[273] Wilson, 66.

[274] Robert P. Carroll, "The Myth of the Empty Land," in D. Jobling and T. Pippin, eds., <u>Ideological Criticism of Biblical Texts</u> (Semeia 59; 1992), 79.

[275] Carroll, 79.

action.²⁷⁶ If it is written, that makes it reality, that makes it history. Those left in the land "presumably did not count." ²⁷⁷ It became an issue of purity. According to Carroll, "purity and emptiness belong together as the prerequisites for the return to the homeland and the rebuilding of YHWH's sacred house."²⁷⁸ There is no mention of what became of the "poorest in the land" who were recruited to harvest the vineyards. Carroll states that "their invisibility or disappearance from the text is not part of the Chronicler's ideology of the polluted and purified Sabbath paying land."²⁷⁹ The strategy to ignore those left in the land denotes the denial of legitimate ownership by those left behind. This supports the notion that any people in the land can be classified as a "polluting force."²⁸⁰

For Carroll, the community behind this controlling force is the second temple community.

> What all the stories taken together seem to be stating in symbolic terms reflects an ideology of occupation and control of the temple community in the reconstructionist era of the Persian period. Not only are there exclusivistic claims to possession of and power in the land, but there is also such a denigration of all opposition that no rival claim has any legitimacy whatsoever. Where once deportation may have been a sign of divine anger and rejection, here it has become a foundational element in the warrants for empowerment in the land (cf. Ezek 11:14-21).²⁸¹

In regards to the "poorest in the land", Carroll states that "they occupy space but that space is purely geophysical, it is not part of the symbolic geography whose ideology underwrites so much of the Hebrew Bible."²⁸² Although Carroll argues that there were other groups in the land, other exiles from earlier deportations, they too were considered unworthy to participate in the inner circle because their return did not take place at the

---

[276] Carroll, 9.

[277] Carroll, 0.

[278] Carroll, 80.

[279] Carroll, 81.

[280] Carroll, 91.

[281] Carroll, 83.

[282] Carroll, 83-84.

right time.[283] Therefore, Carroll is convinced that the second temple community is behind the "myth of the empty land."

> The second temple community was therefore solely the creation of the *benê haggôlâ* or *'am haggôlâ* ("the people of the deportation"), and the sacred enclave belonged only to them. The empty land myth must be seen as the production and property of that group of people, with its original power-base in the imperial court and the creation of the temple community as the forging of a power-base in the Judean territory.[284]

In sum, Carroll's proposal in favor of the myth of the empty land attempts to explain the contradiction of the texts in relation to the number of people involved in the deportations and the situation of the land after the exiles returned. He concludes that because the people in the land were powerless, the Babylonian exiles chose to produce literature and ideologies that would validate their existence as the true Israel and justify their refusal to accept into their restored community anybody remaining in the land.

The "myth of the empty land" theory does not necessarily hold up in Isa 40-55. In the very first chapter (40:9) Deutero-Isaiah proclaims the news of deliverance to those in Jerusalem who in turn are commanded to pass the good news on to the "cities of Judah." This suggests that there were people present to receive the message of comfort. In later chapters Deutero-Isaiah makes mention of "watchmen" (52:8) and sending a "herald to Jerusalem" (41:27). In 51:17, the city, or the people therein, are told to "rouse yourself" and "arise". In 52:1, "Jerusalem, the holy city," is commanded to "put on your robes of majesty". From these examples alone, it seems possible that Deutero-Isaiah recognized an audience in Judah.

Perhaps his primary attention is given to those in exile because they faced the greatest threat of assimilation and apostasy. This gives the reader the impression that those left in the land were somehow unimportant or excluded from the plan of comfort. The exiles were the political, social and religious leaders of Israel. They needed to respond to the message of salvation, thereby validating the significance the message held for them and for all the people of Israel. Deutero-Isaiah's message is very inclusive (49:6) and in his vision, all were invited to respond to the righteousness of God (55:1), not just an elite group of returnees.

---

[283] Carroll, 86.

[284] Carroll, 85.

Norman K. Gottwald

Norman K. Gottwald applies an Eagletonian reading to Isaiah 40-55 in an attempt to identify the social class and the ideology of Deutero-Isaiah. He lays out his intent and strategy from the beginning. The categories Terry Eagleton proposes are the general mode of material production (political economy), the literary model of production, the general ideology, the aesthetic ideology, and the authorial ideology.[285] By using these five categories the text can be read "obliquely" and can produce a unique ideology of the text.

Eagleton stresses two important points in the use of this strategy:

> 1) the text has an integrity of its own since it is no direct transcript of anything else and cannot simply be interchanged with anything outside itself...

> 2) the text exists in a specific space within the larger complex of social life with which it is connected in a variety of ways and, as a result, its very inviolate individuality as text is itself a form of social and ideological production whose full shape we cannot see unless we work to reconstruct the web of social forces at work in the production...[286]

It is Gottwald's purpose "to sketch the web of social forces at their conjuncture in Isaiah 40-55 along the lines of Eagleton's categories, in order to see if this way of looking at the text illuminates it significantly."[287] The categories are as follows:

> 1) *General Mode of Production*. The forces and relations of material production in the Babylonian Empire formed a tributary mode of production in which a strong centralized state dominated an agrarian economy, siphoning off the surplus of the productive populace by means of state taxation and privately controlled rent and debt.... The audience of Isaiah 40-55 was inserted into this tributary mode of production as "neutralized" ex-officials and civil servants of the defunct State of Judah who had been in Babylonian detention for two or three generations.

---

[285] Norman K. Gottwald, "Social Class and Ideology in Isaiah 40-55: An Eagletonian Reading," <u>Ideological Criticism in Biblical Texts</u>, D. Jobling and T. Pippin, eds. Semeia 59 (Atlanta: Scholars Press, 1992), 43.

[286] Gottwald, 43-44.

[287] Gottwald, 44.

world--unrecognized not only by other nations but by the Judahites 2) *Literary Mode of Production.* Under a tributary mode of production literature is not mass produced. It is written by hand, and multiple copies are the exception rather than the rule.... Isaiah 40-55 arises at a point of conflict between two state-formed entities, the one Judahite and powerless and the other Babylonian and all-powerful.... It is highly probable that it was produced and consumed under clandestine and subversive conditions.

3) *General Ideology.* Here we must take "general" on two levels: What was general to the Babylonian tributary mode of production and what was predominant within the community of deported Judahites? ...The Babylonian umbrella ideology was typical of ancient Near Eastern states: the existing order of the state and of society into classes was ordained by cosmic order and in turn helped to maintain cosmic order. Subject peoples such as the Judahites deserved their inferior position as a part of the cosmic-political hegemony... The predominant ideology of the Judahite deportees in Babylon has to be reconstructed from what Isaiah 40-55 says or implies about them, ... My reading is that these deportees by and large held on to their own version of tributary ideology. They saw themselves as privileged representatives of the cosmic-political order once established in Jerusalem.

4) *Aesthetic Ideology.* One important distinction can be made between the Babylonian and general Near Eastern "aesthetic ideology" and the Judahite and general Israelite "aesthetic ideology." Whereas the visual arts are important to the former, the latter focuses on words as the primary carriers of meaning.

5) *Authorial Ideology.* We may summarize that this author is a Judahite ex-official, a master of the cultic and historical traditions of pre-exilic Judah, a gifted rhetorician, a committed Yahwist with an expansive monotheistic outlook, a pronounced Persian sympathizer, and the vocal supporter of an anti-Babylonian political orientation and strategy for his community... I would articulate the commanding authorial ideology as follows: the rise and fall of tributary sovereignties is in the hands of one divine being, the God of Israel who is also the unrecognized God of the as well. [288]

Through the use of Eagleton's categories, Gottwald actually makes a strong, if somewhat different case, for each of the three themes underlying Isa 40-55 addressed in this chapter. First, Gottwald supports the exiles as the main audience in Deutero-Isaiah. He states the following. I regard this section of Isaiah as a coherent whole addressed to Jewish deportees in Babylonia in the period 550-538 B.C.E... The work developed over time in active dialogue and open conflict between author and audience. The aim of

---

[288] Gottwald, 44-48.

the author was to enlist the audience in a program of return to Judah, and that goal was attained at about the time the text was completed. [289]

Secondly, Gottwald argues that the resident Judahites are an insignificant audience to the author of Isaiah 40-55. He further states that "... the role of the Judahites who remained in the land is ignored while the functions of the abolished Davidic dynasty are distributed in part to Judah's Persian overlords and in part to the restored exilic elite." [290]

Gottwald states that there are two possible reasons for the shunning of the people left in the land both by the book of 2 Kings and the Chronicler, as well as Deutero-Isaiah. The first reason is the possibility that Deutero-Isaiah was so far removed from Jerusalem that he did not know what was going on there. Gottwald dismisses this possibility immediately based on the amount of communication that occurred between the exiles and those left in the land as suggested by both the Book of Ezekiel and the Book of Jeremiah, which are, presumably, on the whole somewhat earlier than Deutero-Isaiah. Therefore Gottwald concludes that the second reason is the only plausible one: "The absence is most likely the result of disputed claims to leadership over the Judahite community."[291]

Those in Babylon were given "exilic privilege." They did not care about how the Judahites would react to their return and claims of leadership. They had to welcome it with open arms or "acquiesce in the leadership of the returning elite who will carry the stamp of Cyrus' approval."[292] Therefore, Gottwald concludes the following in regards to the function of Isaiah 40-55 for the returning exiles.

> In short, Isaiah 40-55 in its exuberance for return assumes a politically passive and culturally/religously insignificant populace in Judah, waiting to be shaped by the very descendants of the officials who had led them to ruin in the first place. Thus, we must conclude that in the author's mind, and in the view of his audience as well, the imaginative figures of Jacob/Israel, Lady Zion and the Oppressed Servant of Isaiah 40-55 are supremely, even exclusively, those Judahites who were detained in Babylon.[293]

---

[289] Gottwald, 44.

[290] Gottwald, 43.

[291] Gottwald, 52.

[292] Gottwald, 52.

[293] Gottwald, 53.

Thirdly, Gottwald also agrees with the third theme of this chapter, that the return to Jerusalem is a crucial part of Deutero-Isaiah's plan of action. He views the purpose of Deutero-Isaiah's work as a way "...to instill a sense of mission that will motivate this disillusioned elite to risk participating in a pro-Persian political movement and to lobby for a restoration of the Judahite homeland with itself as the core leadership."[294] Gottwald denotes the return to the homeland as an integral part of the "authorial ideology" component of an Eagletonian ideology. The return to the land validates the sovereignty of God to the nations and Israel's restoration is dependent on that return. So for Gottwald, "The overriding authorial ideology is sharply focused on the prospect of a Judahite restoration by the Persians, and this seems to be based upon a close reading of events in the latter years of the Babylonian imperium."[295]

In sum, Gottwald's use of the Eagletonian ideological criticism leads him to some of the same conclusions reached by the majority of the other scholars discussed in this chapter: the exiles are the major audience, those left in Judah are an insignificant audience due to the political and religious posturing for power and position, return to Jerusalem is pertinent to the task of the Servant for the message of salvation must come from the place where God is particularly present, and finally, the message is inclusive and must be shared with "the ends of the earth."

---

[294] Gottwald, 52.

[295] Gottwald, 49.

Daniel Smith-Christopher

Smith-Christopher's focus in this article is to reassess the social and historical impact of the Babylonian Exile. He dates the period 597/587-539 B.C.E.[296] Smith-Christopher accuses some of his predecessors (Torrey) and current colleagues (Bright, Ackroyd, Raitt, Klein and Foster) of neglecting to place sufficient emphasis on the social and psychological impact the exile had on Israel historically.[297] What is lacking, in Smith-Christopher's opinion, is an "informed perspective on the social, socio-psychological, and therefore, theological impact of the disasters of 597 and especially 587."[298]

Smith-Christopher views the Babylonian exile as a "critically important event in the history and development of the Hebrew people..."[299] He gives a lengthy summary of the historical events leading up to the exile beginning with Assyria and the fall of the northern kingdom. He revisits these events in order to counter any claims that life in exile was comfortable. He especially vehemently opposes those who use the Muras´hu Archives and the Elephantine Colony as evidence supporting a less severe and traumatic experience than he proposes. [300]

Smith-Christopher argues in favor of a devastating experience by those in Judah, one that completely changed their thinking, their behavior and their religion. He cites examples of other cultures having experienced cultural devastation and physical relocation (African-Americans and Native Americans) as evidence of the mental anguish a people experiences when all that they know is taken from them and they are subjected to environmental brainwashing and memory lapses related to their identity and history as a people in a different land. He refers to this analysis as a "sociology of separation and purity."[301]

Smith-Christopher makes "a synoptic observation of the exilic experience" by re-examining Ezekiel's bizarre behavior. Rather than blaming the victim, Smith-Christopher suggests that he may have been

---

[296] Smith-Christopher, 7.

[297] Smith-Christopher, 7-9.

[298] Smith-Christopher, 11.

[299] Smith-Christopher, 8.

[300] Smith-Christopher, 26.

[301] Smith-Christopher, 33.

suffering from psychological trauma as a result of being deported to Babylonia.[302]

Smith-Christopher cites some of the inscriptions from the court of Nabonidus as archaeological evidence revealing the forced military service of the people of "Hatti-land."[303] According to Smith-Christopher, these people were forced to guard King Nabonidus of Babylon. Smith-Christopher supports C.J. Gadd who argued that these were people from "Jewish communities" that are referred to as people of "Hatti-land."[304] He cites another cuneiform inscription, this time referring to Nebuchadrezzar, which reads as follows

> ....the lands of Hattim, from the upper sea to the lower sea, the land of Sumer and Akkad, the land between the two rivers... the rulers of the Lands of Hattim across the Euphrates where the sun sets, whose rulership, at the bidding of Marduk my Lord, I overcame, and the mighty Cedars of the mountain of Lebanon were brought to the City of Babylon, the whole of the races, people from far places, whom Marduk my Lord delivered to me - *I forced them to work* on the building of Etemenanki - I *imposed* on them the brick-baskets...[305]

Smith-Christopher continues to argue that the Jews experienced a great deal of trauma from the exilic experience by reviewing "a brief consideration of selections from the harsh vocabulary of defeat. Chains and bonds are spoken of in at least three different major terms, and frequently associated with the Babylonian conquest..."[306] The three terms Smith-Christopher make reference to are: *mpr* "to tie, imprison"; *zq* "fetter"; *nhst'q* "bronze fetters." In Smith-Christopher's opinion, the "various forms of the Hebrew terms normally rendered "imprisonment" turn up as metaphors for exile..."[307]

Smith-Christopher is convinced that the trauma of exile was so severe that it profoundly effected the behavior of Israel through the post-exilic

---

[302] Smith-Christopher, 32.

[303] Smith-Christopher, 28.

[304] Smith-Christopher, 28.

[305] Smith-Christopher, 24.

[306] Smith-Christopher, 28.

[307] Smith-Christopher, 29.

God Comforts Israel

period. For although Cyrus conquered Babylon, for Israel, that just meant a different oppressor. Smith-Christopher makes this point to emphasize the continued trauma suffered by the exiles.

> Part of the myth of Persian benevolence is the idea of an "end" to the exile in 539. But all that "ended" was Neo-Babylonian hegemony, to be replaced by that of the Persians. Ezra would point out, in his public prayer, that the Jewish people were "slaves in our own land" under the Persians (Neh 9:36-37). "Post-exilic Hebrew writings, like Daniel, would go so far as to reinterpret Jeremiah's predicted "70 years" into 490 years, effectively implying that the people were *still* in exile in the Persian and Hellenistic periods.[308]

This is also seen in the Ezra-Nehemiah emphasis on mixed-marriages.

> Furthermore, it is clear that the exilic, and particularly post-exilic, community reveals the typical behavior patterns of a minority community that has closed ranks tightly to maintain identity and faith. The social emphasis on separation in the mixed-marriage crisis of Ezra-Nehemiah reveals a traumatized community that is often blamed for "closed-mindedness" by modern commentators.[309]

In sum, Smith-Christopher is determined to revisit first, the level of anguish and suffering Israel encountered from her enemies during the eighth and seventh centuries B.C.E. and, secondly, the particular effect the destruction of their land and the relocation to Babylonia had on Israel from a social and psychological perspective. His recollection of the history of Israel's suffering at the hands of her enemies serves as a background of just how devastating the final blow of 587/86 B.C.E. was to the people who believed they would always be in the land of their ancestors and under the rule of a Davidic king.

Smith-Christopher's purpose is to remind the critics of the exile of this history and to encourage the scholars of today to take more seriously the whole picture of the exile, not just the theological fallout which tried to explain why it occurred in the first place. Instead, Smith-Christopher presents the exiles as a hurting people in grave need of comfort, hope and restoration.

---

[308] Smith-Christopher, 22-23.

[309] Smith-Christopher, 35.

Summary

In this chapter we have examined eleven prominent scholars--seven are commentators and four are authors of studies on Isaiah 40-55. There is some consensus among all eleven scholars studied: 1) the primary audience is in Babylonian exile; 2) Jerusalem is the place to re-gather and experience God's restoration; 3) Israel is called to be the "servant" whose task is to bring salvation to the nations; 4) the nations are called to participate in the new salvation of God.

However, the confusion and different opinions become evident when an attempt is made to interpret the identity of the audience as they are addressed in the text. This is especially seen in the two major parallelisms: Zion/Jerusalem and Jacob/Israel. Here the scholars vary in opinion and the multitude of opinions all seem to find validity in the text itself.

The eleven scholars fall into two schools of thought. The first school of thought views Isaiah 40-55 as addressing the people as a whole nation. Included in this school of thought are Westermann, Whybray, Knight and Baltzer. They stress the point that the Babylonian exiles are the primary audience but they do not exclude those in Judah, whether Judah is a symbol or an actual audience. Since the chapters address the city of Jerusalem and "all the cities of Judah," these scholars conclude that the whole nation is addressed in Deutero-Isaiah's message of comfort.

The second school of thought dismisses the Judeans as a significant audience. It is the Babylonian exiles (and perhaps all the exiles scattered in Diaspora) that need to return to Jerusalem for an identity affirmation, restoration and comfort. This school of thought includes the majority of those examined in this chapter. Included are, Clifford, Brueggemann, Hanson, and Wilson. One reason given for this almost exclusive focus of Deutero-Isaiah is that the Babylonian exiles were facing the greatest threat of assimilation and apostasy.

The second group of scholars (Gottwald, Carroll, Wilson, Smith-Christopher) are more focussed on the sociological, political or religious perspectives of chapters 40-55. Their use of these modes of interpretation help to clarify the possible meaning these chapters may have had for their original audiences.

CHAPTER 3

THE AGENDA OF COMFORT IN DEUTERO-ISAIAH

The agenda of Deutero-Isaiah involves finding a way forward for the people of God who have collectively witnessed--and themselves precipitated--the destruction of Judah and Jerusalem and the exile of thousands of the leaders of Judah. Granted, the actual audience for Deutero-Isaiah is constituted primarily by people not yet borne in 598/597, 587/586, but the collective memory is dominant. The agenda is three-fold. First, God declares to the people that they will be comforted by God (40:1; 49:13; 51:3,12; 52:9; 54:11). This comfort includes forgiveness for past sins and a reaffirmation of their position as the people of God. This is stated at the very beginning in which God as it were commands God to comfort the people and announces the coming return of God to Zion/Jerusalem. The self-command takes the form of plural imperatives addressed to the divine council.

> Comfort ye, oh comfort ye, My people, says your God.
> Speak tenderly (pl) to Jerusalem, and declare (pl) to her
> That her term of service is over, that her iniquity is expiated.
> For she has received at the hand of the Lord double for all her sins.
> 40: 1-2

> But now thus said the Lord -
> Who created you, O Jacob, Who formed you, O Israel:
> Fear not, for I will redeem you;

> I have singled you out by name, you are Mine.
>
> 43:1

Secondly, Deutero-Isaiah's agenda dictates a new role for Israel to play as the Servant of God. This new role entails two aspects: 1) a departure from Babylon and return to Jerusalem/Zion, the proper base for the role of the Servant (43:8; 48:14,20; 49:9; 52:11; 55:12); 2) God's word of comfort and salvation must go forth to the nations from Zion/Jerusalem (44:26,28; 46:13; 55:5), where God is uniquely present.

> I am bringing my victory close;
> It shall not be far,
> And my triumph shall not be delayed.
> I will grant triumph in Zion
> To Israel, in whom I glory.
>
> 46:13

> Turn, turn away, touch naught unclean
> As you depart from there;
> Keep pure, as you go forth from there,
> You who bear the vessels of the Lord.
>
> 52:11

Israel's task as servant is clearly stated in Deutero-Isaiah.

> I, the Lord, in My grace, have summoned you,
> And I have grasped you by the hand.
> I created you, and appointed you
> A covenant people, a light of nations -
> Opening eyes deprived of light,
> Rescuing prisoners from confinement,
> From the dungeon those who sit in darkness.
>
> 42:6

> And now the Lord has resolved -
> He who formed me in the womb to be His servant -
> To bring back Jacob to Himself,
> That Israel may be restored to Him.
> And I have been honored in the sight of the Lord,
> My God has been my strength.
> For He has said:
> "It is too little that you should be My servant
> In that I raise up the tribes of Jacob
> And restore the survivors of Israel:
> I will also make you a light of nations,
> That My salvation may reach the ends of the

earth."

49:5-6

Thirdly, these texts, as well as others, provide some insight into the new agenda for Israel to execute, an agenda to be carried out in the time of the new messiah, the Persian king, Cyrus, who will aid the return.

Declaration of Comfort

The most common Hebrew word that refers to *"comfort"* is *nhm*. It occurs 108 times in the verbal form in the Hebrew Bible (48 niphal, 51 piel, 2 pual, 7 hithpael).[310] The root *nhm* occurs 13 times in Isaiah 1-39 and 8 times in Deutero-Isaiah. The meaning varies throughout the Old Testament. Heinz-Josef Fabry says the following in regards to the frequent use and various translations of *nhm*.

> The only element common to all meanings of *nhm* appears to be the attempt to influence a situation: by changing the course of events, rejecting an obligation, or refraining from an action, when the focus is on the present; by influencing a decision, when the focus is on the future; and by accepting the consequences of an act or helping another accept them, or contrariwise dissociating oneself emotionally from them, when the focus is on the past.[311]

This is in agreement with Deutero-Isaiah's method of persuasion. Deutero-Isaiah consistently attempts to comfort his audience by persuading them that God is sovereign and that because the idol gods have no actual power, they have nothing to fear (44:6-8). This is part of the prophet's focus on the present. Deutero-Isaiah also focuses on the future when he discusses their release as an event about to happen (51:3,11). Then he refers to the past when God admits that God had abandoned them temporarily because of their past sins, but is now about to return to Zion/Jerusalem (40).

> The agenda of comfort is clearest when *nhm* is used in the nipal and piel. The twin factors of decision/effect and emotion/affect are thus the rule in *nhm;* they are indissolubly interwoven, even when in individual cases there may be greater emphasis on one element or the other. Furthermore, the niphal and piel make it possible to emphasize, the alteration of the subject with regard to a specific situation and the subject's determination to

---

[310] Heinz-Josef Fabry, "___" in Theological Dictionary of the Old Testament, ed. G. J. Botterweck et al; trans. David E. Green, (Grand Rapids:Eerdmans, 1998), 342.

[311] Fabry, 342.

change someone else's attitude with regard to the situation.[312]

The piel form is found eight times in Deutero-Isaiah (40:1; 49:13; 51:3, 12; 52:9) and the pual once (54:11). However, the pual continues the message that is promoted in the piel. As a matter of fact, "the pual...exhibits no meaning distinct from the piel apart from its inherent passive sense. Zion and the inhabitants of Jerusalem are (or are not) comforted."[313] Using Fabry's argument in regards to the meaning of *nhm* in the piel, one can argue that Deutero-Isaiah's comfort agenda is used to change the attitude of all his listeners (the nations, the exiles, the Judahites, the Babylonians). The piel form of *nhm* "expresses Yahweh's comforting of the people as a group whenever it's found in the prophetic texts."[314] Therefore, when Deutero-Isaiah addresses the groups found in chapters 40-55, the message is that God's wrath has turned into comfort and that God brings comfort to Israel first, then to the ends of the earth. This understanding of God as the comforter became the distinct meaning of the usage of *nhm* in the piel.

> Dieses ausgepragte Verstandnis liegt nun uberall da vor, wo Jahwe selbst der Troster ist, denn in seiner Zuwendung zum Trost erneuert Gott die Gnaden- gemeinschaft mit dem, von dem er sich im Zorn abgewandt hat... Von hier aus ist die Bedeutung verstandlich, die *nhm* pi. in der Verkundigung Deuterojesajas gewinnt....[315]

Fabry concurs with Stoebe and states the following. More common is the clear statement (verb in the perf.) that Yahweh has comforted his people (Isa 49:13;52:9) or Zion (Isa 51:3 [twice]) or the certainty that Yahweh will comfort Zion (Zec. 1:17).[316]

H. Van Dyke Parunak includes in the description of the usage of *nhm* the prelude of punishment, God's jealously for Zion and God's displeasure

---

[312] Fabry, 342-43.

[313] Fabry, 352.

[314] Fabry, 352.

[315] H. J. Stoebe, "___", Theologisches Halndworterbuch zum Alten Testament, eds. Ernst Jenni and Claus Westermann (Zurich: Kaiser Verlag Munchen Theologischer Verlag, 1976), 62.

[316] Fabry, 351.

with Israel's enemies when they attempt to oppress God's people.³¹⁷ It is God's sympathetic pain or compassion that lies at the heart of the biblical motif for comfort according to Parunak.³¹⁸ He finds evidence in support of his argument in the parallelism of *nhm* in the Piel and Pual with the noun form, and also by the twofold sense of *nhm* as both comfort and compassion.³¹⁹

The Agenda of Comfort for Israel

1) 40:1

> Comfort ye, oh comfort ye, My people, says your God.
> Speak tenderly to Jerusalem, and declare to her
> That her term of service is over, that her iniquity is expiated;
> For she has received at the hand of the Lord
> Double for all her sins.

The verb form of *nhm* used in this verse is second person masculine, plural, imperative. Since the verb is plural, most scholars believe God is speaking to the Divine Council of Yahweh.³²⁰ The Divine Council is told to announce the forthcoming comfort. Deutero-Isaiah's message of comfort in 40:1 is meant to counter the fear that God has abandoned Israel and that the enemies of God's elect will permanently overcome them. So the word "comfort" is used here to denote relief from the suffering and oppression Israel experienced at the hands of the Babylonians. It is a comfort that can only come truly from the divine realm. Its purpose is to announce God's forgiveness and God's return to Zion after a brief absence. Paul Hanson states the following about God's absence and presence.

> The passage with which Second Isaiah opens his proclamation is about divine absence and divine presence. Israel knew what absence was about, having served its term like a prisoner removed from people and places Israel loved. Israel had been incarcerated in the gloom of warfare and desolation and hopelessness. In the bitterness of its laments, Israel had asked whether

---

[317] H. Van Dyke Parunak, "A Semantic Survey of NHM", <u>Biblical 56</u>, (1975), 515.

[318] Parunak, 517.

[319] Parunak, 517.

[320] Knight, 7; Whybray, 48; Clifford, 72; Brueggemann, 16; Hanson, 18

God cared any longer.[321]

The message of comfort in 40:1 is that no less an authority than God announces that they are forgiven.

2) 49:13

> Shout, O heavens, and rejoice, O earth!
> Break into shooting, O hills!
> For the Lord has comforted His people,
> And has taken back His afflicted ones in love.

Chapter 49 is so dramatically different from chapters 40-48 that some scholars divide Isa 49-55 from Isa 40-48. These scholars note that Cyrus is not mentioned in this section and that Zion is used here to refer to a new restored Israel.[322] Chapter 49:13 follows the second Servant Song (49:1-6). The Servant's task, which is to facilitate the restoration, is laid out in v 8: to (re)establish the land; to (re)assign the desolate properties; to free those "imprisoned", to bring into the light those in darkness; to make provisions for their needs as they journey back to the land .[323]

According to Westermann, comfort in this context means "intervention to put an end to extremity".[324] The meaning here is similar to 40:1. The comfort is offered and now needs a response. A response must come from Israel and all the nations, so now Deutero-Isaiah includes all of creation! With this open invitation of praise, this hymn of praise stands out from vv 1-12. Because of the obvious hymnic style of vs 13, some scholars isolate vs 13 as a hymn. However, this is not the case for Brueggemann who includes

---

[321]   Knight, 25.

[322]   James Muilenburg, "Second Isaiah", Interpreters Bible. Vol. 5. Ed. George A. Buttrick et al, 422-652. (New York: Abingdon Press, 1962), 564; Westermann, 28; John D. W. Watts, Isaiah 34-66. Word Bible Commentary, Vol. 25, ed. David A Hubbard et al   (Waco: Word Book, 1987), 72; Knight, 125; Clifford, 6; Whybray, 137; Hanson, 12-13; Brueggemann,112; Baltzer, 304; Brevard Childs, Isaiah (Lousiville: Westminster John   Knox Press, 2001), 372-73; Chris Franke, Isaiah 46, 47, and 48 A New Literary-Critical   Reading (Winona Lake: Eisenbrauns, 1994), 249.

[323]   Hanson, 132-33.

[324]   Westermann, 216.

vs 13 with verses 14-26.[325] Brueggemann identifies vs 13 as a hymnic affirmation with the purpose of summoning all of creation to sing the praises of God who is about to bring comfort to Zion.

> The summons is that the whole cosmos might sing in praise of Yahweh. The reason is that Yahweh has "comforted" and had "compassion" on Israel. The cosmos is to celebrate the comforting of Israel! The first verb, "comfort," echoes the initial announcement of forgiveness in 40:1. The second verb, "have compassion" (as in v. 10), reflects the attentive concern of a mother for a child.[326]

For Brueggemann "the cause for cosmic rejoicing is the revival of Jerusalem."[327]

Knight argues that this verse is a reflection on the fall of Babylon.[328] According to Knight, the fall of Babylon has become a "greater incident than the redemption of all the Hebrews scattered amongst the nations."[329] He supposes that liberation from Babylonian exile and the return of God's people to Zion is the ultimate testimony of the sovereignty of God. But Knight points out the irony of an "afflicted people" now called to be "the instrument of the Holy God's salvation to the rest of the world." According to Knight, Deutero-Isaiah identifies Israel as an "afflicted people" because of her deserved punishment. Through her affliction Israel becomes transformed for it is no longer Israel's action that is primary, but the Word of God. This Word now bears the consequences of Israel's guilt. This is what gives occasion for the heavens and the earth to bring forth praise.[330] In Knight's opinion, the call for the heavens and the earth to rejoice can not be passed off as just sentimental poetry. Instead he argues that "the Hebrews employed poetry along with the parable as a vehicle to convey truth at those moments when no prose language could do so."[331]

---

[325] The following authors isolate vs. 13: Westermann, 216; Whybray, 142; Hanson, 126; Baltzer, 318. Brueggemann, 115.

[326] Brueggemann, 115.

[327] Brueggemann, 116.

[328] Knight, 135.

[329] Knight, 135.

[330] Knight, 136-37.

[331] Knight, 135.

In Baltzer's opinion, the hymn in vs 13 is meant to contrast the far-reaching power of God over against the Persian imperial ideology.[332] Baltzer states that this hymn is proclaiming God as Lord over the entire polytheistic environment. Because the mountain is a symbol of Sinai-Horeb where God's revelation was made manifest to Israel, and God's association with Zion/Jerusalem, Baltzer concludes that his hymn is a confession of faith which links the Exodus with the Babylonian exile.[333]

> Horeb, and the exodus from The first exodus from Egypt, the revelation of the law on Mount Sinai-Babylonian exile are all linked together in a confessional formula. That is liberation and compassion for the poor. This is lament and jubilation simultaneously, in remembrance...of the "Servant without a name," Moses.... But God continues to have compassion on his poor and wretched human beings.[334]

.3) 51:3

> Truly the Lord has comforted Zion,
> Comforted all her ruins;
> He has made her wilderness like Eden,
> Her desert like the Garden of the Lord.
> Gladness and joy shall abide there,
> Thanksgiving and the sound of music.

Comfort in this context appears to refer to the land and the coming transformation that is about to take place. For Westermann the meaning of comfort is clear. He finds that "the repetition of 'Yahweh has comforted' makes it perfectly plain that in Deutero-IsaiahI 'comfort' means a turning towards a person that definitely alters a distressful situation, and not just words of sympathy."[335] If Westermann's definition of comfort is correct, then the message in this text is that God has now turned God's face back towards Jerusalem and this turning will not only alleviate the problem, but bring restoration so great that it can only be compared to the Garden of Eden. Hanson differs from Westermann's position. He expands the unit to 51:1-52:12. For Hanson one gets a greater sense of Deutero-Isaiah's

---

[332] Baltzer, 318.

[333] Baltzer, 318.

[334] Baltzer, 318.

[335] Westermann, 237.

structure and thematic unity if the larger unit is read together.[336] This unit is filled with imperatives that give direction to Deutero-Isaiah's audiences on how to respond to the message of comfort. They are told to "rouse yourself," "awake," and "Depart" (51:9,17; 52:1,11). There are three audiences addressed in this unit according to Hanson: God (51:9-10), Jerusalem/Zion (51:3) and the exiles (51:1-2,4-8).[337] This unit seems to provide a summary of the several components of Deutero-Isaiah's message of comfort: the re-establishment of election status is mentioned through the names of Abraham and Sarah (vv 1-2), the restoration of the land (v 3), the release from captivity (vv 5-6), the return of the diaspora (v 11), the recognition that God is sovereign (vv 9-16); the mention of forgiveness (vv 17-23). Hanson sees the message of comfort in this unit in the following way.

> Consistent with the first verse of his call (40:1), Second Isaiah realizes that the principal word he is commissioned to bring to this anxious community is a word of divine *comfort*. The comfort he brings is not a facile, well-intentioned human word of sympathy but a powerful assurance that verses 12 and 13 contrast the earthly oppressor 'who fades like grass' with the Creator of the heavens and the earth....The challenge he brings is this: 'Do not forget, remember!.' Remember that the one who determines the future is the God simultaneously creating the universe and loving his creatures, at once 'stretching out the heavens....' and saying to Zion, 'You are my people' (51:16).[338]

Hanson's view was already expressed by James Muilenburg.

---

[336] Westermann, 143.

[337] Westermann, 143.

[338] Westermann, 147.

The unity of this poem, which is denied by the great majority of contemporary scholars, is shown by the persistence of its dominant theme throughout: the comforting of Zion by the repeated assurance that the time of her deliverance is at hand....An examination of the prophet's diction strongly reinforces the impression gained by the unity of the theme: deliverance; salvation; joy and gladness; comfort.[339]

John McKenzie sees a connection between the restoration of the land and the mention of Abraham and Sarah. He states that when Israel was only Abraham and Sarah, Israel could not perceive the promise that it would one day be a great nation. For McKenzie, Deutero-Isaiah is appealing to history as a motive of faith.[340] God's promise to Israel will issue in a transformation of the land of Judah.[341]

Whybray sees these verses somewhat differently. He cuts the unit off at 51:1-8 and sees the major audience as those exiles who were discouraged but tried to remain faithful to God.[342] Whybray argues that this audience is concerned that they are too small a number to go back to Jerusalem and do all the restoration on their own. He bases this argument on the reference to Abraham and Sarah in vs 2, the recipients of God's promise to make Abraham a great nation.[343] These verses respond to the concern that God will do the restoration and God will bring forth others to assist the people/ Servant Israel, in their work.

George Knight brings out some very interesting points in this text. He places great emphasis on the mention of Sarah in vs 2, the only other time she is mentioned outside of Genesis. The mention of Sarah (who was barren) is essential to the metaphor of progeny and to Deutero-Isaiah's argument proclaiming the blessing of a multitude that will return to Jerusalem. For Knight, Deutero-Isaiah is telling the people that God will do for Zion what God did for Abraham and Sarah, who fathered them and gave birth to them.[344]

---

[339] Muilenburg, 589.

[340] McKenzie, 125.

[341] McKenzie, 125.

[342] Whybray, 154.

[343] Whybray, 155-56.

[344] Knight, 151.

4) 51:12

> I, I am He who comforts you
> What ails you that you fear
> Man who must die,
> Mortals who fare like grass?

According to Muilenburg, this verse emphasizes that God alone has the power to comfort, no one else.[345] Hanson stresses that 51:9-11 is a "poetic gem" and directs the attention of the audience backward to a time even before Abraham and Sarah.[346] Hanson focuses on the fear element of the text and how this fear is responsible for their amnesia.

For Hanson, fear leads to forgetfulness, which in turn leads to loss of identity and despair. This despair banishes hope and creates chaos.[347] The fear is eliminated when the audience embraces the power of God. To be without fear is to receive comfort. Therefore, 51:12 adds this new characteristic to the message of comfort: fear leads to forgetfulness and must be avoided. Comfort replaces fear and only comes from God. Whybray is similar to Hanson in his analysis of the element of comfort in this text.

> Here, as in 40:1, 'comfort' is not just a matter of speaking soothing words, but of bringing the nation's suffering to an end. The remaining of these two verses goes to the root of the exiles' despairing cry of verses 9-10: they have failed to understand the true meaning of their own traditional faith. For them the activity of Yahweh has been confined to the past; yet it ought to be obvious to them that his creation of the world implies an unchallenged and continuing mastery over the universe beside which **man who dies and who is made like grass** is of no account at all. Fear of **the fury of the oppressor** consequently shows a lack of faith. So Yahweh turns the tables: it is not he who has **forgotten** his people (cf. 49:14), but they who have **forgotten**: to fear men is to forget God.[348]

Therefore, it appears that the meaning of comfort in this text is not to

---

[345] Muilenburg, 598-99.

[346] Hanson, 146.

[347] Hanson, 151.

[348] Whybray, 160.

fear mortals but to remember God's activity in the world. The connection between fear and comfort is also lifted up by Baltzer. Baltzer states that "in the present text the argument is based on the transience of human beings, and especially rulers and their power. Fear of other human beings is misplaced. God is not mortal: he "ruleth on high, almighty to save," as the hymn says." [349]

5) 52:9

> Raise a shout together, O ruins of Jerusalem!
> For the Lord will comfort His people, will redeem Jerusalem

Westermann points out that Deutero-Isaiah alludes to the tidings, not the details of the return because "this enables him to avoid any delineation of the actual return itself, and what he says remains completely concentrated on God's part in the act."[350] Deutero-Isaiah's purpose is to announce and to prepare the people for what is happening and will happen in the immediate future. The command here is directly addressed to the "waste places" of Jerusalem. Westermann states that the "waste places" represent "the suffering, bewildered and weary remnant of the nation in exile and the Diaspora."[351] McKenzie states that it is an "allusion to the cosmological myth in which the deity slays the monster of chaos."[352] Hanson agrees with McKenzie and states the following.

> As not infrequently in the Bible, we here find echoes of this mythic drama. In 51:9-10 the battle against the chaos monster Rahab was described. In verses 51:7 and 52:1 Jerusalem/Zion was summoned to rouse herself and prepare herself for a celebration of victory by clothing herself in beautiful garments. The celebration itself breaks forth in 52:7-10 with the announcement to Zion that the victorious God has returned to the capital city. True to the universal scope of the ancient pattern, the victory is witnessed by all nations, for the restoration thereby accomplished affects the ends of the earth (52:10).[353]

---

[349] Baltzer, 361.

[350] Westermann, 249-50.

[351] Westermann, 251.

[352] McKenzie, 123.

[353] Hanson, 149-50.

Comfort can thus be understood in this unit (52:10) as the restoration of Jerusalem's waste places (v 9), the return of the Lord to Zion (v 8), and the satisfaction of knowing that the nations who were once their oppressors will now be witnesses to the salvation of God (v 10).

6) 54:11

> Unhappy, storm-tossed one, uncomforted!
> I will lay carbuncles as your building stones
> And make your foundations of sapphires.

Westermann discusses this verse as part of the unit 54:11-17, which he divides into two parts--vv11-13a and vv 13b-17.[354] The first section describes the new Jerusalem in all her glory. The second part gives the assurance of peace and security for the future.[355] Zion is addressed as "O afflicted One," a title we also find in 51:21. This address brings to mind the lamentations brought forth immediately after the destruction of Jerusalem (Lam 1:3,9; 3:1,19). Deutero-Isaiah also describes this audience as "not comforted" (54:11). Again, the author of Lamentations expresses his pain and the suffering of his people, as well as the condition of the city, as "none to comfort her" (1:2,17,21) and having "no comforter" (1:9). This sentiment is being expressed again here in Isa 54:11.

Earlier in 54:7-8 God states that God had for "a brief moment forsaken the people," and for "a moment hid my face from them," but with compassion God promises to again gather them up into his fold. Thus Isa 54 appears to be a letter of assurance and a promise of restoration to all the audiences of God's intent to provide comfort. Chapter 54:11b deals with buildings and their restoration, a topic Deutero-Isaiah does not focus on anywhere else in his work. The whole theme is the glittering splendor of Jerusalem's buildings.[356] It appears that Deutero-Isaiah is attempting to bring to the reader's mind the vast destruction of a city that was once known for its splendor, majesty and glory.

Perhaps Deutero-Isaiah remembers the complaints. However, in the past the mention of such splendorous buildings was condemned by the prophets, except in regards to the temple.[357]

---

[354] Westermann, 276-77.

[355] Westermann, 277.

[356] Westermann, 277.

[357] Westermann, 278.

For Westermann, this means that Jerusalem will be God's city in a way completely different than before, as the city's glittering splendor points directly towards the divine majesty of God.[358] It is God who will design the new city and draw up the plans for its restoration. In Westermann's opinion, Deutero-Isaiah is describing the salvation of God.[359] McKenzie interprets the verse differently from Westermann. He argues that Isaiah 54 is about the community of the redeemed and God's enduring love.[360]

> The promises to Zion now reach a point of magnificence that goes beyond any mere historical reality of the restoration of Jerusalem. The point of the imagery is that Yahweh is founding a lasting city, one that will not again suffer the fate of the Jerusalem of the monarchy.... But the vision of the prophet here approaches the eschatological; the lasting city of Yahweh's good pleasure is not a material reality of walls and buildings located at a definite point of longitude and latitude; it is a community of the redeemed, of all those who are 'instructed of Yahweh' and are 'established in righteousness.' Such a community will outlast any material structure in which it happens to be incorporated at a given moment of history. This is the indestructible Jerusalem which no enemy can harm. The righteousness of Yahweh is a foundation stronger than any material foundation, proof against any human effort, even the effort of those who dwell in Jerusalem to corrupt it.[361]

Hanson argues more along the lines of Westermann in interpreting the statement as an earthly reality, not an eschatological image.

> Verses 11-12 picture God's preparation of Zion for the return of the faithful people. The restoration of God's people is not a fuzzy abstraction. As stated so clearly by a later visionary architect, 'the home of God is among mortals' (Rev 21:3). The covenant people will sing their praises within a real-life context, a city adorned and protected by God.[362]

The message of comfort found in 54:11 has one focus - the restoration of the city. It is a direct response to the laments about the condition of the city

---

[358] Westermann, 278.

[359] Westermann, 278.

[360] McKenzie, 137.

[361] McKenzie, 140.

[362] Hanson, 173.

after the conquest and the audience's appeals for restoration and renovation. Deutero-Isaiah assures the people that the city will be rebuilt and that it will be even more beautiful than before. No one will again come up against her and be victorious, for no weapon formed against it shall succeed (54:17).

The Return to Zion/Jerusalem

The Babylonian captors were not especially brutal to the Israelites, as were the Assyrians. As noted above, the Judaean exiles were probably allowed to build homes, plant crops, marry and own businesses. This may suggest that comfort was offered to the exiles on some level from the Babylonians. Yet there is some question about their ability and freedom to practice their own religion to the specifications of the covenant laws and in exclusion of the local idols. Certainly they had no temple for a focal point. Then there is the issue of being on foreign soil so far away from Judah. Sociologists of disaster report the lasting effect of these events on the memories of the victims, "especially when they come in series of disasters."[363] Smith-Christopher states the following in his analysis of the effect the exile had on those in exile.

> Once we understand the importance of crisis, we can process an analysis of the kind of crisis that the Exile represented. As can be seen in our historical reconstruction, the Exile represented military defeat and continued military domination, which daily reminded them that they were no longer an independent people. Furthermore,...deported to Mesopotamia, the crisis added the further dynamic of a minority consciousness that continued to create social conflict among those in Exile as well.... the awareness that the exiles were among "foreigners" ...continued to be a legacy of the Exile long into the Intertestamental literature...[364]

The range of comfort in Deutero-Isaiah promises deliverance from captivity (43:8; 48:20;49:9; 52:11-12; 55:12) and a pleasant journey home (40:4;41:17-20; 49:9-11; 55:12-13). Richtsje Abma states the following in regards to the return to Zion.

> Within DI chs. 49-55 starts a new episode, as 48.20-22 announces: 'Go out from Babylon, flee from Chaldea... say: "Yhwh has redeemed his servant Jacob!" In the next chapters the call to leave Babylon is repeated (49.9; 52.11) and the journey of the returning people is described (49.22-23; 51.11; 52.12). The main theme of these chapters is no longer the situation in

---

[363] Smith-Christopher, 19.

[364] Smith, Religion of the Landless, 53.

Babylon but the return to Zion.[365]

Abma argues that the possible return to Zion did not find unanimous enthusiasm, but that there was a great deal of conflict and hostility around this issue.

> This points to an important theme in the following chapters: the call to leave Babylon meets with different reactions, including resistance. Accordingly Isaiah 49-55 shows that the return to Zion is not a smooth operation but an enterprise with obstacles and hardship. The experience of hardship is especially connected with the work of the servant of Yahweh.[366]

Abma divides chapters 49-55 into ten parts in an attempt to identify the location of the text. For Abma, there are two locations - Babylon and Zion. By examining these texts so identified (Babylon: 49:1-6; 7-13;14-26; 50:1-3;4-11; 51:1-16; 52:11-15; 55:1-13; Zion: 51:17-23; 52:1-10) Abma concludes that there are two conflicting parties who are the main audiences--those in Jerusalem who are not receptive to the return of the first group of exiles, and those remaining in Babylon who refused to go back and help in the rebuilding of the city.[367] Amba views these chapters as a drama (see Baltzer and Watts) and as written in Judah during the fifth century.[368] The purpose of the drama of chapters 49-55 is three-fold. First, the drama is supposed to convince those in Babylon to leave and "join in the restoration of Zion."[369] Second, "during the drama Zion moves from her humiliated and desolate state into a queenly position. This effect is attained by Yahweh, who reaffirms his bond with Zion and takes up his residence in her midst."[370] The third and final purpose of chapters 49-55 is the focus "on the servant of Yahweh and his opponents. During the drama the servant experiences the ultimate humiliation from his oppressors but in the end the

---

[365] Richtsje Abma, "Traveling from Babylon to Zion: Location and its function in Isaiah 49-55", JSOT 74, 1997, 6.

[366] Abma, 6-7.

[367] Abma, 23.

[368] Abma, 28.

[369] Abma, 25.

[370] Abma, 26.

victory is his."³⁷¹ In conclusion, Abma says the following.

> The crucial matter is whether Israel will follow Yahweh and his servant and undertake the return to Zion so that the comfort of Zion becomes full reality....The double address to Zion and Babylon serves this goal exactly. It is an ingenious man oeuvre that directs the attention of the people in Babylon to Zion and in fact functions as an invitation to the people to make the movement that the text itself makes: to travel from Babylon to Zion. ³⁷²

The plan for release and return are made even more clear in 49:9 according to Whybray.

> After this brief glimpse of the ultimate result of Yahweh's plan for the exiles, a more detailed picture is now given of the stages by which it is to be carried out: first, the release of the exiles from Babylon....then the miraculous journey through the desert from Babylon to Palestine....³⁷³

Whybray continues to compare chapter 52:11-12 to the Exodus event of release and departure.

> The exiles are to take with them on their journey the sacred temple vessels removed by Nebuchadnezzar (2 Kg. 25:14-15) which had, it seems, been carefully preserved in Babylon (Ezra.1:7-11; 5:14-15). The journey thus has the character of a solemn religious procession, necessitating ceremonial purity...³⁷⁴

Anderson finds the similarities between the first Exodus and the Exodus theme dispersed throughout Deutero-Isaiah.

> The new event not only surpasses the old; it supersedes it in many respects. Thus the prophet traces elements of contrast between the old and the new exodus. In Moses' time the fugitives had to celebrate the Passover in haste...., but of the new exodus it is said: "you shall not go out in haste"...; for Israel shall go out in joy and be led forth in peace (55:12). Unlike the old exodus, there will be no terrors or dangers along the way, and the people, instead of murmuring, will march with a faith that breaks forth into hymns of praise, the music of which will be taken up by the mountains and

---

³⁷¹ Abma, 26.

³⁷² Abma, 27.

³⁷³ Whybray, 141.

³⁷⁴ Whybray, 168.

the hills. The new exodus will be accompanied by a new covenant, but not like the old contractual covenant of Moses. Second Isaiah avoids mention of the Mosaic covenant...and instead, with a theocentric emphasis, turns to the "everlasting covenant"...made with David... Here, however, the *berît 'ôl_m* is not made with a member of the house of David, but with Israel (55:3), and is analogous to the permanent covenant made with Noah after the Flood (54:9-10).[375]

Clifford argues that the departure from Babylon and the return to Zion is paramount to the plan of comfort.

The last command is to bring the people forth (43:8). The impression given is that to move back to Zion is to take part in creation and to remain in Babylon is to yield to the domination of chaotic, anti-community forces. The prophet, eager to lead his people, puts before them the fundamental choice - to remain static or to move.[376]

In Clifford's opinion the people are called to act. This action leads to departure from Babylon and exultation of God's power.

The imperatives of vv. 20-21 summon them to action. Leave the city of the no-gods with exultation appropriate to a victory by Yahweh! Their talk to each on the way is to be of their redemption. The prosperity and righteousness promised in v. 18bc will be felt even in the infertile desert as they journey to the land of promise, v. 21.[377]

Clifford further comments on the theme of departure found in 52:11-12.

Vv. 11-12 are a coda, urging all to leave Babylon portrayed as a new Egypt through the citation of the rare word used of the old Exodus, "in haste." Exodus 12:11 has said "and you shall eat it [the Passover lamb] in haste." No need to fear. Yahweh is about to lead the stately and secure procession back to Zion. In this entire speech one sees the pastoral plan of the prophet. The people are to believe that their Lord can overcome their oppressors and lead them home to a Jerusalem restored to queenly dignity.[378]

---

[375] Bernhard W. Anderson, "Exodus Typology in Second Isaiah", <u>Israel's Prophetic Heritage: Essays in honor of James Muilenburg</u>, eds. Bernhard W. Anderson and Walter Harrelson (New York: Harper and Brothers, 1962), 191.

[376] Clifford, 99.

[377] Clifford, 145.

[378] Clifford, 172.

Westermann views 48:20 as a hymn of jubilation which includes the summons to "go forth from Babylon!" He argues that the actual event is anticipated as a coming reality.[379] It has not yet taken place. "Nevertheless, the strains of jubilation at both are to be raised right away, in order that the prophet's word of salvation....may be re-echoed in the answer of the community, its responsory."[380]

Then in 52:11-12 Westermann argues that "the command to depart is that to which the entire message of Deutero-Isaiah has been leading up."[381] However, he does not believe that these verses are a literal description of departure from Babylon. Rather, in his opinion, its intention is to stress the need to separate from that which is unclean.[382]

Christopher Seitz argues that a concern over the people's return to Zion is the center of Deutero-Isaiah's work.

> The point is: Second Isaiah addresses the topic of the fate of Israel's dispersed, together with a concern over Zion's destiny... The perspective is Zion-centered, in geographical and theological terms, even as the material shows great concern with the fate of the dispersed and of their return to Zion. By the same token, the introduction speaks of *God's* return to Zion - a return that will transform Zion as wilderness into Zion as fertile land. It is on this note that Second Isaiah concludes (55:13).[383]

Hanson interprets the meaning of 48:20 as a literal command to get out of Babylon!

> The culminating summons and invitation in verses 20-21 indicate, however, that the people are not to get mired in self-pity but are to take the preceding instructions as a call to immediate obedience and response. The command is specific, it is bold, and it has tremendous political, economic, and personal implications. The people are to break up their households, pull up their roots, pack up, set forth from Babylon in unwavering trust that God has already acted...[384]

---

[379] Westermann, 204-5.

[380] Westermann, 205.

[381] Westermann, 252.

[382] Westermann, 253.

[383] Christopher Seitz, <u>Zion's Final Destiny</u>, (Minneapolis: Fortress Press, 1991), 206.

[384] Hanson, 125.

Hanson's comments on 49:9 are more poignant about the need to return. He argues "there is nothing theoretical about the Servant's assignment. It involves restoration of confiscated property, release of political prisoners, and provision for their needs as they travel back to their homes."[385] Hanson stresses again the importance of Israel's return as mentioned in 52:11-12. Here, Yahweh has already returned to the city. But the city is in exile! Therefore, the drama is not complete until the exiles return. For Hanson, "the people must march back to their homeland."[386]

Walter Brueggemann's entire argument for understanding Deutero-Isaiah's message is based on the theme of "homecoming." Brueggemann sums up the theme of Deutero-Isaiah in his introduction.

> ... for in the end the book of Isaiah is an oratorio about the *suffering and destiny of Jerusalem*. The city is regarded as the center of Yahweh's peculiar attentiveness as the seat of the world's best hopes for well-being, and as the site of the most profound disobedience and recalcitrance... It is Jerusalem that is imagined healed, restored, ransomed, forgiven (65:18-19). It is Jerusalem, the meeting place of divine will and historical reality, that is the recipient of Yahweh's judgment and Yahweh's renewing comfort and mercy.[387]

Brueggemann ties the theme of deliverance from Babylon to the redemption of Israel. The command to "go out" in 48:20 is an Exodus verb. It is meant to remind the exiles of the Exodus experience. The departure from Babylon is just one step towards Israel's redemption. Upon her departure, Israel is to proclaim a special message: "Yahweh has redeemed Israel...That is who Yahweh is, consequently, that is who Israel is - Yahweh's redeemed and emancipated!"[388] Brueggemann continues this line of argument in 49:9 by identifying the verb "come out" as another Exodus verb.

> The verb "come out" is an exodus verb, asking the Babylonian exiles to leave the thralldom of Babylon as their ancestors left the certitudes of Egypt (see 52:11)...The work of the servant is to enliven the exilic community with new intentionality and courage that will eventuate in homecoming, a life outside the contours of the empire.[389]

---

[385] Hanson, 132-33.

[386] Hanson, 150.

[387] Brueggemann, 2.

[388] Brueggemann, 107.

[389] Brueggemann, 114.

Brueggemann views the work of the servant as going beyond ministering to the Babylonian exiles. The servant must summon all the "scattered of the earth." Brueggeman emphasizes that "the work of the servant as shepherd is the *gathering of the scattered* (see v.5; Jer 31:10). The scattered are in many places. They shall now come home from everywhere they have been scattered, from all directions (v.12)."[390]

Brueggemann again acknowledges the use of "Exodus language" in 52:11-12. He places great emphasis on the use of six imperatives in these verses ("depart, depart, go out, touch, go out, purify"). Yet, for Brueggemann, this text is even more concerned about the liturgical aspect of departure.

> Because the return is liturgical and will come to the presence of God, Israel must take care to stay pure. The final verb seems to allude especially to the priests who perhaps lead the procession and who carry in liturgical style the very temple accouterments that were seized and confiscated by Babylon (see 2 Kings 25:13- 17). The return envisioned here is not military and political, but it is liturgical. Israel will be a religious community whose life is properly focused on right worship.[391]

Anderson, Knight, Brueggemann, and Hanson agree in regards to Deutero-Isaiah's intentional use of "Exodus language." Anderson connects the new exodus with the restoration of Zion and the offer of salvation to the "ends of the earth."

> The fall of Babylon would be followed by a new exodus, more marvelous than the Exodus under Moses, and by the restoration of Zion. This new event would prompt the whole world to recognize that Yahweh is God alone and that his salvation extends to the ends of the earth. It is significant that Second Isaiah's prophecy begins (40:3-5) and ends (55:12-13) with the theme of the new exodus. Indeed, the poems as a whole are largely variations on the Exodus tradition.[392]

Knight argues that the departure from Babylon must be understood in terms of the Exodus event.[393] The purpose for using the "Exodus language" is to remind the people that God could do it again. Therefore the logic is that

---

[390] Brueggemann, 114.

[391] Brueggemann, 140.

[392] Anderson, 182.

[393] Knight, 123.

"if God had done this before, then he could easily do it again, and do it for a people who would have to face the desert once again on the homeward road to Zion (cf Exod. 17: 6; Num. 20:11; Ps. 105:41; and already at Isa. 41:17-18)."[394]

For Knight, the thread of inclusivity is ever present in the theme of departure and redemption. "The redemption of Israel is thus bound up with the redemption of others through Israel.[395] In Knight's opinion, "Deutero-Isaiah sees the exiles returning not just from Babylon, but from every point of the compass."[396] Part of Servant Israel's task is to bring redemption to "the peoples who lived at the ends of the earth and the redemption of Israel was to reach to the ends of the earth."[397]

Finally, Knight continues to argue that inclusivity is a major part of Servant Israel's task in 52:11-12. Exiles everywhere are called to take part in the great Exodus, for they "are summoned to recognize their original calling to be a kingdom of priests and a holy nation." [398]

The Message of comfort must come from Jerusalem

The place from which this word of comfort must be proclaimed is Zion/Jerusalem. Zion/Jerusalem represents a disconnection from seats of imperial power and emphasizes the unique connection of God to the place Zion/Jerusalem. A return marks a vindication of God's continuing special relationship with Israel. Brueggemann makes the following comments on the importance of "land" to the people Israel.

> The "land" for which Israel yearns and which it remembers is never unclaimed space but is always *a place with Yahweh*, a place well filled with memories of life with him and promise from him and vows to him. It is land that provides the central assurance to Israel of its historicality, that it will be and always must be concerned with actual rootage in a place which is a repository for commitment and therefore identity.[399]

---

[394] Knight, 123.

[395] Knight, 134.

[396] Knight, 134.

[397] Knight, 134.

[398] Knight, 164.

[399] Walter Brueggemann, The Land. (Phil: Fortress Press, 1977), 5-6.

There are three theses used by Deutero-Isaiah that support this argument. The first thesis states that the exiles are being released to live out the salvation of God in Jerusalem, not in Babylon. It is a message that cannot be received from a place of bondage. For in order for the message to have effect, power and witness, it must come from the place where the people had been in covenant relationship with God--Jerusalem (43:10, 12;44:8; 52:1,8,9; 55:5). Babylon is a symbol of God's defeat and Jerusalem's destruction. The promises made to Abraham, Noah and David, are all null and void to this second and third generation audience as they sit in the cities of Babylon. Psalm 137:5-6, probably uttered by the first group of deportees, expresses the need to remember Jerusalem and its meaning for them as God's people.

> If I forget you, O Jerusalem,
> let my right hand wither;
> let my tongue stick to my palate
> if I cease to think of you,
> if I do not keep Jerusalem in memory
> even at my happiest hour.

The exiles need to have a new experience with God from Jerusalem. Those in Diaspora are also being called back to Zion/Jerusalem (43:6; 49:12, 22-25; 51:11; 54:2,3) to take part in this new experience. This is the destination of the new people of God.

> So let the ransomed of the Lord return,
> and come with shouting to Zion,
> crowned with joy everlasting.
> Let them attain joy and gladness,
> while sorrow and sighing flee. 51:11

Brueggemann describes the need to be in Zion/Jerusalem in this way.

> By the power and the mercy of God, this community of faith will very soon be led back to the "holy land" where the values of the Torah tradition are not resisted but in fact received and practiced as normative and true. It is a deep yearning in this faith community of exile to be in the only place where those values are presumed. For good reason that place is "home."[400]

Brueggemann views the place Zion/Jerusalem as "safe space" away from the temptation and apostasy of the "fleshpots of Babylon and Persia." In

---

[400] Walter Brueggemann, Hopeful Imagination. Prophetic Voices in Exile (Phila: Fortress Press, 1986), 94.

Zion/Jerusalem the returnees can be reconnected to their past and the traditions that define their being and identity. Even during the exile, Jerusalem was the place where the exiles could direct their prayers in "assurance that YHWH would still be available, that prayers could still ascend on that sacred mountain."[401] It was believed that Jerusalem, as the sacred city, "is the conduit through which messages pass from earth to heaven, no matter where, in a geographical sense, they originated." [402]

Seitz argues that Zion's final destiny is focused on her restoration.

> The theological "provenance" of the literature is the divine council (40-48) and Zion-Jerusalem (49-55). God will gather the dispersed like "lambs in his arms" (40:11). God will bring them to Zion, as God returns. Second Isaiah is concerned with the return of exiles, from all compass points, to a restored Zion. [403]

Little is said about the mechanism Deutero-Isaiah will use to bring his vision to fruition. For according to Ackroyd, "Deutero-Isaiah's prophecies are much more concerned with the larger questions of the understanding of the present situation and prospect of a new act of deliverance than with the details of the return and restoration itself."[404] However, Ackroyd does admit that there are some allusions that show Deutero-Isaiah's expectations.

> But there is sufficient allusion to show that he, too, like Ezekiel, thought in terms of a new land, and that the idea of a restored land involves for him the idea of a complete renovation of the natural order. The fertility of the land will be assured ... (40:1ff; 41:17-20,cf. ch.35; 49:19ff.; 51:1ff; 55:12f.). It will be a new people...., re-established in a new covenant relationship with God (cf. 55:3-5; 54:9-10; 42:6; 49:8). Jerusalem will be consoled and rebuilt and the cities of Judah...will be restored (44:24-28), with Cyrus as the agent of this rebuilding (45:13). The population will increase in a city refounded and built with precious stones (54:11-14), a city of righteousness, freed from all fear. Here the new people will be found, with a picture of the purity of the new city, and an assurance of the continued blessing of God upon the people (cf. ch. 52). At every point, these themes are interwoven with the

---

[401] Jon D. Levenson, <u>Sinai and Zion: An Entry into the Jewish Bible</u>. (San Francisco: Harper and Row, 1985; 1987, 125.

[402] Jon D. Levenson, 125.

[403] Christopher Seitz, 206.

[404] Peter Ackroyd, <u>Exile and Restoration</u> (Phila: Westminster, 1968), 135.

larger concerns of God's action, so that the inter-relationship between restoration in the physical sense and restoration of the inner life of the people is never lost.[405]

The second thesis found in Deutero-Isaiah in regards to the message of salvation coming from Jerusalem instead of Babylon, is that Zion/Jerusalem is the place to which the presence of God has returned.

> Ascend a lofty mountain, O herald of joy to Zion;
> Raise your voice with power, O herald of joy to Jerusalem
> Raise it, have no fear;
> Announce to the cities of Judah: Behold your God!
> 40:9

> Hark!
> Your watchmen raise their voices,
> As one they shout for joy;
> For every eye shall behold
> The Lord's return to Zion!
> 52:8

The underlying theme of God's return to Zion/Jerusalem permeates the entire book of Deutero-Isaiah. God does not live in exile, but has only temporarily turned away from the people living there because of their sins.

> For a little while I forsook you,
> But with vast love I will bring you back.
> In slight anger, for a moment,
> I hid My face from you;
> But with kindness everlasting
> I will take you back in love
>   - said the Lord your Redeemer.
> 54:7-8

Snaith argues that the return from Babylonia is the primary theme of Deutero-Isaiah.

> The prophet did not set out to state his doctrine of the Servant, nor did he set out to write a treatise on monotheism... He had but one theme on this list: the Return. His task was to convince the Judean exiles that the return was certain and that it was increasingly imminent. He had to open their blind eyes and make them see this. The prophet's insistence on the uniqueness of the God of Israel is his main confidence in the Return. This is why he

---

[405] Ackroyd, 135.

emphasizes God's incomparable majesty and power, and His effectiveness against the ineptitude of the idols of Babylon. But the Return is not proof of the unique power and might of God. Rather, the unique power and might of the ONE GOD is the guarantee of the Return. The prophet begins with the Return; he ends with it; he deals with it all the time in between. Everything in the nineteen chapters has to do with it, and everything is subordinate to it. This is his theme: the Return from the Babylonian exile, involving the resurrection as from the dead of the old Israel, and the resurgence as from a new birth of a new Israel. [406]

The returnees from the ends of the earth must now gather in the place where God's presence abides if they are to be re-established as the new people of God, with whom the nations will join (God's peculiar place--not a temporary imperial capital). God's presence in Jerusalem is a part of a very ancient tradition that connects God's presence with the actual city. This is part of the Zion tradition that is found primarily in the Psalms and in Isaiah of Jerusalem.

Ben C. Ollenburger argues that Zion is a theological symbol and therefore, cannot be placed in one configuration, but was "capable of evoking more than one response."[407] This appears to be the case for Deutero-Isaiah who uses the term Zion frequently throughout, but more so in the latter chapters. Ollenburger points out in his monograph "that Zion as an iconic vehicle has among its denotations the kingship of Yahweh, and among its connotations Yahweh's exclusive prerogative to be the defender of and to provide security for his people."[408] This plays out well in chapters 40-55.

Deutero-Isaiah uses the disputation and the trial speech to show that God is the sovereign King of the universe and to prove that the idol gods of Babylon are nothing.

> The things once predicted to Zion -
> Behold, here they are!
> And again I send a herald to Jerusalem.
> But I look and there is not a man;

---

[406] Norman H. Snaith, "Isaiah 40-66: A Study of the Teaching of the Second Isaiah and its Consequences," in <u>Studies on the Second Part of the Book of Isaiah</u>, Supplements to Vetus Testamentum, Vol. XIV, ed. G.W. Anderson et al. (Leiden: E.J. Brill, 1967), 149.

[407] Ben C. Ollenburger, <u>Zion The City of the Great King</u> (Sheffield: JSOT Press, 1987), 18.

[408] Ollenburger, 19.

> Not one of them can predict
> Or can respond when I question him.
> See, they are all nothingness,
> Their works are nullity,
> Their statues are naught and nil.
> 41:27-29

Perhaps the notion of Yahweh as Israel's King (43:15; 52:7), the acceptance of Persian imperial rule; the abdication of an independent political regime under a Davidic king, explains why Deutero-Isaiah does not promote a Davidic king in the restoration, but instead divides the kingship duties between Cyrus (45:1) and the people (55:3). If this is the case, then the Zion tradition probably is in the back of Deutero-Isaiah's mind.

The second part of Ollenburger's argument in his investigation of the use of the word Zion as symbol, states that Yahweh has an "exclusive prerogative to be the defender of and to provide security for his people."[409] The exiles have accused God of having forsaken them (40:27; 49:14) or having divorced their "mother" (50:1). Yet God has rebuked their claims or explained His absence (42:24; 49:15; 50:1d; 52:3; 54:7-8). As the sole defender of Israel against the nations, God has played the role of the *go'el* throughout Deutero-Isaiah. Evidence for this is found in the several passages where forms of *go'el* are used; a) God as redeemer (41:14; 43:1; 44:6,24; 48:17; 49:7,26, 54:8); b) Israel as the redeemed (43:14; 44:22; 51:10; 52:9; 54:5).

> Fear not, O worm Jacob,
> O men of Israel:
> I will help you
>   - declares the Lord -
> I your Redeemer, the Holy One of Israel.
> 41:14.

Clearly, Deutero-Isaiah had the Zion tradition well in mind when addressing his audiences. He has appealed to other traditions to persuade his audiences to accept their forgiveness and to return to Zion/Jerusalem (Abraham/Sarah; Noah; Exodus; David).

Ollenburger's argument provides an interesting and creative avenue for interpreting the effect the Zion symbol has for Deutero-Isaiah's agenda. From the very beginning (40:2) Deutero-Isaiah makes it clear that Zion/Jerusalem is first to hear the message of comfort from the Divine Council. He later argues that it is the place where God's people must congregate and accept their new task as the Servant of God.

---

[409] Ollenburger, 19.

J.J. Roberts' analysis of Deutero-Isaiah's use of the "Zion Tradition" differs slightly from Ollenburger. Roberts states the following.

> Second Isaiah also develops his understanding of Yahweh's special relationship to his people through use of the Zion tradition, but he supplements that tradition by appeal to the creation, exodus, and patriarchal traditions. This prophet of the exile follows First Isaiah in attributing the present plight of Jerusalem to Yahweh's purging judgment, brought on by Israel's sins (40:2; 42:24-25; 48:10). Nonetheless, Yahweh has not forsaken his people or deserted his city forever. The great king will return to his city, and Babylon, the agent God used to punish Jerusalem, will in turn feel the fury of God's wrath because she showed no mercy and misunderstood her real role in God's plan (47:1-7). Zion will be glorified, and the nations will stream to her, escorting her children back in honor (49:22; 51:3; 54:11-17).[410]

God's Word of Comfort is for Israel and the Nations

The third and final thesis of Deutero-Isaiah in regards to the task of Israel as the Servant of God is that the message of salvation is offered not only to Israel but is now being offered to all flesh. Melugin states the following in regards to 40:1-11.

> Isa 40:1-11 as a whole proclaims comfort to a Jerusalem that has suffered for her sins, a new exodus brought forth by the mouth of Yahweh, the commissioning of a message-bearer, and instructions to a tidings-bringer as to what to do and say. The object of deliverance is Jerusalem; it is she who will be the beneficiary of the new exodus. Yet the result of Jerusalem's deliverance and Yahweh's rule is the revelation of God's glory (v.5). And the manifestation of Yahweh's glory has worldwide significance: it is beheld, not only by Israel, but by "all flesh." The salvation of Jerusalem is not an end in itself; it leads to the recognition of Yahweh's glory by all flesh.[411]

Therefore, from the very beginning of Deutero-Isaiah's message, inclusivity has been the intent. Simon, who dates Deutero-Isaiah at 400 B.C.E., says the following in regards to Deutero-Isaiah's message of inclusivity.

---

[410] J.J.M. Roberts. "Isaiah in Old Testament Theology", Interpreting the Prophets (Phila: Fortress Press, 1987), 71.

[411] Roy F. Melugin, "Israel and the Nations in Isaiah 40-55", Problems in Biblical Theology:Essays in Honor of Rolf Knierim, eds Henry T.C.Sun, Keith L. Eades, James M. Robinson and Garth I. Moller (Grand Rapids: Eerdmans, 1997), 252.

The real Isaiah, however, ought to be placed later, at about 400 B.C., when he broadly and deliberately attacks the narrow schools of Judaism and the paganism of the Greek world and invites all, Jews and Gentiles, in Palestine and everywhere to accept salvation on a transcendental scale.[412]

The nations function as a group in Israel's theological speech. According to Brueggemann, "One aspect of that God-other engagement that is typical of Israel's theological speech is God in relation to the nations."[413] The God of the Old Testament is a God "who deals with the nations, and the nations inescapably deal with the God of Israel. Together they form a common subject in Israel's theological speech."[414] The identity of the nations is not revealed in Deutero-Isaiah. Orlinsky argued that all expressions such as "nations", "ends of the earth" and "peoples" refer only to Babylonia.[415] He based his argument on the political environment at that time. No other nation (Egypt, Phoenicia, Edom, Philistia) could compare to the might of Babylon.[416]

Baltzer agrees with Simon and suggests that "nations" refer to the Greek speaking countries of Asia Minor.[417] What is important for Deutero-Isaiah is that salvation is now offered to the "nations" as part of the task of the Servant Israel.

> For He has said:
> "It is too little that you should be My servant
> In that I raise up the tribes of Jacob
> And restore the survivors of Israel;
> I will also make you a light of nations,
> That My salvation may reach the ends of the earth."

---

[412] U.E. Simon, A Theology of Salvation (London: SPCK, 1953), p. 16.

[413] Walter Brueggemann, "At the Mercy of Babylon: A Subversive Rereading of the Empire", A Social Reading of the Old Testament (Minneapolis: Fortress Press, 1994), 111.

[414] Brueggemann, "At the Mercy of Babylon..."111.

[415] H. M. Orlinsky, "The So-Called 'Servant of the Lord' And 'Suffering Servant' in Second Isaiah", Supplements to Vetus Testamentum XIV Studies On the Second Part Of the Book of Isaiah. (Leiden: E.J. Brill, 1967), 32.

[416] Orlinsky, 32.

[417] Baltzer, 89.

49:6

The key phrase here is "light of nations." Deutero-Isaiah uses the phrase "light to the nations" twice (42:6; 49:6) and "light to the peoples" once (51:4). These three verses will be examined in an attempt to show that part of Israel's task as Servant is to extend an invitation of salvation to all of God's people.

In 42:6 one finds the phrase following the first Servant Song (42:1-4). The Servant is validated by God as the one whom God has chosen and as one in whom God's soul delights (v. 1). Deutero-Isaiah leads up to the meaning of the Servant's role as "a light to the nations." In verses 5-7 Deutero-Isaiah parallels the phrase with "I have given you as a covenant to the people." This seems to suggest that the meaning of "light" in this context is the law and covenant that God made with Israel's ancestors and is now renewing with the present generation. Westermann says the following about the Servant's mission as a "light to the nations."

> One thing is certain: the words, 'I make you as,' mean that the person addressed is destined to become a tool or means whereby God effects something on others. This is shown by the second part of the verse. 'I make you the light to the nations,' which means, 'through you the nations are to experience light, illumination and salvation.' Then, taking the two phrases as parallel, *berit 'am* supposedly means, 'I make you the covenant-salvation (that is, the salvation given in the covenant) for all humankind.' [418]

Paul Hanson makes a different observation regarding these verses. For Hanson, the focus is not mainly on the law but on the responsibilities of the Servant as the called community of God. It is the task of the Servant as community, to give witness to the nations.

> Isaiah 42:5-8 gives the appearance of an addition provided by a disciple of Second Isaiah who wanted to make explicit one of the important interpretive possibilities implicit in the rich symbol of the Servant....The community called and upheld by God, by discharging the patient faithful witness assigned to the Servant, becomes the instrument through which the nations are drawn into the covenant relationship marked by God's reign of justice, the covenant relationship of which Israel already had been a part because of God's gracious activity on Israel's behalf and which now was to be extended to the wider family of the nations. The parallel phrase "a light to the nations" amplifies this vision, that is, Israel is to become the instrument through which nations come to share the light of God's salvation.[419]

---

[418] Westermann, 97.

[419] Hanson, 46-47.

God Comforts Israel

Hanson further describes the implications of this task for the nations.

> Lest the vision be left in suspension like a glorious icon for decorative purposes only, verse 7 goes on to give specificity to the implications of the covenant as it reaches the nations. It makes clear that the order of God's justice involves healing of human illness and the reform of oppressive political structures. As God's covenant with Israel took shape in the form of God's actively getting involved in the plight of slaves in Egypt, so too the task of the servant people involves advocacy for those who suffer and are oppressed.[420]

For Melugin Israel's mission to the nations is related to the David and Zion traditions.

> Thus Deutero-Isaiah and Trito-Isaiah were not tied to one tradition as a vehicle for expressing the "mission" of the covenant people to the nations. Moreover, the ancient traditions are used rather freely: e.g., the Davidic tradition is "democratized" to apply to the whole people.... The kind of figure commissioned there remains ambiguous. The obscurity is probably intentional. The prophet freely used the images of David and then of Zion to express Israel's mission to the nations; 42:5-9 is but one more example of his freedom.[421]

The Servant who has been called is given the distinct task to share "light" with the whole world which in turn will establish God's justice or *mispat*. The world's acceptance of the *mispat* of God will establish comfort throughout the earth and permit order to conquer chaos.

Isa 49:6 is the second reference to the Servant's role as "a light to the nations." In this text God decides to expand the mission of the Servant beyond the re-establishment of the tribes of Jacob and Israel. God announces that the Servant will be given as a "light to the nations." Ackroyd argues that the task of the new people of God is to make known the purpose of God to the ends of the earth.

---

[420] Hanson, 47.

[421] Roy F. Melugin, The Formation of Isaiah 40-55 (Berlin: Walter de Gruyter, 1976), 68.

> Just as in Ezekiel the nations are the witnesses of what has happened, so that the name of Yahweh is glorified, so, too, in Deutero-Isaiah the purpose of Yahweh is made known through Israel. The limit of God's purpose is not reached in the restoration of Israel, but in the extension of his saving power to the ends of the earth (49:6)...The exaltation of the servant of God brings in the nations as the witnesses in amazement at what God has done (52:13-53:12)... Her restoration will be a recovery of that Zion which is the place of God's dwelling, as central to the life of the world (cf. Isa:2:1-4 =Micah 4:1-4).[422]

Melugin argues along the same lines and states that this style of commissioning is created by Deutero-Isaiah to emphasize the servant's mission to the world.

> A study of the opening to the poem adds to the contention that the speech reflects as much Deutero-Isaiah's creativity as it does traditional form. The summoning of the nations in a report of a commissioning appears only here. It was common in Israel's hymns to call the nations to praise; on other occasions the nations were summoned in connection with judgment against Israel, to hear a song, or a wisdom teaching.... In Isaiah 49:1, Deutero-Isaiah incorporated a summons to the nations into the servant's report of his commissioning because he wanted to emphasize something not conventionally expressed in traditional forms of such reports; he wanted to emphasize that the servant's mission is directed to the nations.[423]

Being a "light to the nations" reveals the very inclusive intent of Deutero-Isaiah's message. In this text we find evidence that the agenda for comfort was meant first for Israel in exile, who in turn will bring it to Zion/Jerusalem, and secondly for the nations and ultimately, all creation. But if Israel as God's Servant is "blind and deaf," how can Israel provide light to others? All that is required is to embrace their God and hearken to God's word (55:1-3). So the light in 49:6 does not only confirm the coming restoration of Israel and the tribes of Jacob, but the whole world.

Muilenburg interpreted 49:1-6 as a sign of Israel's mission being extended beyond the confines of her own people.[424] In v.4 the Servant laments that he has "labored in vain," probably a reference to the resistance he experienced from some of the groups in exile who were opposed to his message. But rather then lighten his load, God has extended his responsibility to include the nations.

---

[422] Ackroyd, 136-37.

[423] Melugin, 71.

[424] Muilenburg, 569.

The third and final text that uses the metaphor of light to describe Israel's new mission is Isa 51:4.

> Listen to me, my people,
> and give ear to me, my nation;
> for the law will go forth from me,
> and my justice for a light to the peoples.

Here we have a slightly different phrase, "light to the peoples." Westermann suggests that the key to understanding this poem (which identifies as 51:1-2, 4-8; along with 50:10-11) is to note that there are three different groups addressed in the three strophes.[425] He identifies the groups in this way: 51:1 and 50:10 are addressed to the proselytes; 51:4 are addressed to the heathen; and 51:1-2, 7 are addressed to the chosen people.[426] He makes the following statement in regards to his position.

> The second strophe addresses the peoples. They, too, are summoned to hear and give heed. The reason given for this in v. 4b is a paraphrase of what the Servant says in 42:3f. about his task for the nations; v. 5b is almost word for word the same as 42:4. This strophe addressed to the peoples is a striking example of the way in which the servant songs lived on and were handed down. The post-exilic community - or a section within it - took up the possibility of salvation for non-Israelites which 42:1-4 had opened up, and in the Servant's name proclaimed to the heathen that Yahweh's salvation was available for them, and that the light which they had been awaiting was now there.[427]

Hanson takes issue with Westermann's conclusions on the grounds that he has divided the thirty-five verses (50:1-52:12) into dozens of separate units and fragments. For Hanson the composition taken as a whole is what gives it a "powerful sense of structural and thematic unity."[428] Hanson does agree with Westermann that the inclusivity of the phrase "light to the peoples" is meant here to bring comfort and to encourage Zion.

The second section (51:4-6) suggests that together with the third Servant Song the first also may have been in the mind of the prophet as he

---

[425] Westermann, 232-34.

[426] Westermann, 234.

[427] Westermann, 235.

[428] Hanson, 143.

composed this lesson. The circle of those addressed has been widened from those "that pursue righteousness/seek the Lord" to "my people/nation." And the commission they receive is the one the Servant received in 42:1-9, to extend God's justice/ light/ teaching to the nations.[429]

The Servant's role as a "light to the nations/peoples" involves the justice and law of God. It is open to all peoples from all nations and its salvation is everlasting. It is not enough that Israel returns to Zion. Once there, as the Servant of God, Israel must proclaim God as God of all the earth (54:5) and Lord of Hosts (45:13; 47:4; 54:5). Israel's restoration will amaze the nations who thought Israel had been defeated and wiped off the face of the earth.

Summary

The agenda of Deutero-Isaiah is focused on bringing comfort to Israel first, then to those in the Diaspora. Ultimately, the nations and all creation are included. This is seen in the several texts that engage the word *nhm*, "comfort" to reveal the various meanings and objects of God's comfort. The interpretation of *nhm*, is broad. God's forgiveness begins the process of comfort and the people must respond. It includes forgiveness and a return to the elect status; to be without fear of the idol gods of their oppressors; restoration of the "waste places"; the return from Babylon and the journey to Zion/Jerusalem for all those in Diaspora; and finally, promoting a new indestructible Jerusalem founded on the righteousness of God.

Yet, as God's new people they are given an even greater task that includes both offering salvation to the other nations and serving as advocate for those who suffer and are oppressed. This must all be accomplished from the Holy City --Jerusalem. Jerusalem is the place where God's presence dwells according to the royal Zion tradition. It is the place of the Torah and where the values of the Torah tradition can be disseminated. In Jerusalem they are reconnected to their past experiences with God--from the Exodus up until now. God has already returned. God awaits the return of His Servant people who will accept the task of witnessing and responding to the word of salvation.

They are called to participate in the rebuilding of Jerusalem. A Davidic king is not in the vision. The duties of the human king are to be redistributed between Cyrus of Persia and the people themselves. For God has reclaimed the position of King of Jacob (41:21), King of Israel (44:6), and Lord of

---

[429] Hanson, 145.

Hosts (45:13; 47:4; 54:5). Ultimately, God is "God of all the earth" (54:5).

CHAPTER 4

CONCLUSION

This research has attempted to discover the audience and reveal the many dimensions of the message of comfort found in Isaiah 40-55. However, before drawing conclusions, it would be helpful to first provide a summary of what has been developed in the earlier chapters.

Three foci have undergirded this research: 1) the historical/archaeological evidence for the context of Isa 40-55; 2) the identification of the various audiences with reference to the opinions of several key commentators regarding those audiences; and 3) multiple features of the agenda of comfort found in the message of Deutero-Isaiah. The existing studies of the events leading up to the exilic period were influenced mostly by the following biblical accounts: 2 Kgs 24-25; 2 Chr 36:5-21; Ezek; Jer 29,39,52. In addition, only limited archaeological data was available. Based on the then available data, some scholars, such as Torrey (1910), even denied that any exile of the magnitude described in the biblical texts ever occurred.[430] Nonetheless, for centuries the biblical accounts have been the primary data used to obtain clarity in regards to the message and audience of Deutero-Isaiah. More recently, however, additional evidence has come to hand.

We first focused on the historical and political circumstances that shaped the exilic situation found in Deutero-Isaiah. The biblical texts as noted above, present the situation in Judah as dismal and the land as lying in rest/abandonment (2 Chron 36:19-21) because of the sins of the people (Jer

---

[430] C.C. Torrey, "The Exile and the Restoration," in Ezra Studies (New York: Ktav, 1910/1970), 285-340.

35:15-17). We are told that all, or virtually all, the significant people were taken into exile, leaving the "poorest in the land" who were left behind to harvest the vineyards for Nebuchadrezzar (2 Kings 25:12). An attempt to regroup in Mizpah under the Babylonian constituted administration ended in the murder of the appointed governor, Gedaliah, and the self-imposed exile to Egypt of many of those remaining (and probably nearby areas as well). The texts indicate at least three major deportations times (598/97, 587/86, 582 B.C.E.). Nebuchadrezzar's attack in 587/86 was the most devastating to the land and to the inhabitants of Jerusalem. The temple was destroyed, the leadership taken into captivity and the land left in ruins. Some areas north of Jerusalem, for example in Benjamin, remained intact, perhaps because they surrendered early on to the Babylonian army.

The biblical account has found greater support in recent archaeological data as analyzed by Stern. Earlier studies did not have the benefit of this recent data, therefore, especially in the last 20 years, some scholars had seriously questioned the validity and motive of the biblical accounts. This skepticism gave rise to Carroll's theory of "the myth of the empty land," a position that argues against the biblical texts that report that there were no people left in the land.[431] This argument is based on the assumption that those in Babylonian exile created this myth as a way to validate their return to leadership and ultimately, repossession of the land. Gottwald used somewhat different arguments to support Carroll's theory. For Gottwald the discrepancy in population count was the returning Babylonian exiles' way of claiming "exilic privilege."[432] These theories are one way of explaining the contrast between the report of the Chronicler, which states that no people were left in the land and that the land laid hallow, and the 2 Kings account, which suggests that some people were not taken into exile but left to continue the harvest. The group that was left in the land, it is believed, eventually reorganized and took over the homes and vineyards of those taken to Babylon.

---

[431] Robert P. Carroll, 81.

[432] Norman K. Gottwald, 52.

The work of archaeologists, such as Kenyon and Barkay, supports the theory that Jerusalem was generally destroyed and thus essentially uninhabitable. The first century Jewish historian, Josephus, and the modern Assyriologist, D.J. Wiseman, citing extra-biblical sources, also support the accounts of destruction given in the biblical texts. This research is in agreement with the archaeological data that undergirds the biblical accounts and that conclude that the land was basically empty and lying in ruins. This condition was interpreted as a sabbath for healing and forgiveness.[433] E. Stern has provided persuasive data that supports the theory that there was a lack of Babylonian presence in Jerusalem during the exilic period. Although there is evidence of continued occupation in the wider area of the (former) Kingdom of Judah, especially towns north of Jerusalem which some scholars take for evidence for Jerusalem itself (Daniel-Smith Christopher, Barkay, Mazar, Berquist), the city of Jerusalem and points south (e.g. Lachish) were not reoccupied until the later Persian period.[434] Stern's archaeological conclusions support his premise that almost all the cities lay in ruins by the end of the Babylonian period.[435]

The situation of Babylonian exile was examined, noting that there is little data to determine the actual circumstances which those taken to Babylonia encountered. Some information can be deduced from Ezekiel, who was exiled in the first deportation in 598/97 B.C.E. Jeremiah's letter to the exiles before the disaster of 587/86 B.C.E. encouraged those in Babylon to make the best of a bad situation (Jer 29:4-7). Deutero-Isaiah's disputations and trial speeches suggest that exilic life in Babylon was perhaps most challenged in the area of religion and worship practices. The Neo-Babylonian administrative documents record rations given to Jehoichin and

---

[433] 2 Chron 36: 21.

[434] Barkay, 364-65; Berquist, 15; Smith-Christopher, "Reassessing the Historical and Sociological Impact of the Babylonian Exile...", 20; Mazar, 548.

[435] Stern, 309.

his family thereby implying recognition of the Jewish community. The biblical texts do not cite physical oppression.

According to Ezekiel the exiles lived in communities in the area, such as the Chebar Canal (3:15). Archaeological sites such as Tel Melah and Tel Harsha give evidence of habitation by exiled Jews. Although their freedom had some restrictions, Daniel Smith-Christopher argues that they did not become slaves as we know slavery in America, though they knew psychic oppression.[436] Hayes and Miller state that "the Jews preserved some communal cohesion and national identity and may have formed their own ethnic corporations in various towns."[437] According to Ezek, some priests and elders took over the leadership in Babylonia (Ezek. 8:1; 14:1; 20:1, 3). It is believed that "transferred peoples could continue to practice their national religion in the land of their exile, although there was also the tendency to combine this with some form of worship of the gods of the lands in which they dwelt (Ezek. 14:3; 20:29)."[438] The religious status of the exiles can be summed up as consisting of a nonsacrificial cult which promoted prayer, psalms of praise and lamentation, and the reading of the law. In addition, "sermons: may have been preached.

Included in the historical section is the Egyptian Gola--those who fled from Mizpah for fear of retaliation from Nebuchadrezzar for the murder of Gedaliah. Jeremiah was forced to join this group. They arrived at Tahpanhes, an Egyptian outpost in the eastern delta of Egypt bordering Sinai, a site believed to be Tell-ed Defenneh. The Elephantine archives provide interesting similarities between a later Jewish community at the southern boundary of Egypt in the fifth century and the contemporary Jewish community in Jerusalem.

In conclusion, we find a picture of a defeated people who once lived in Judah and Jerusalem but who now are scattered throughout the nations. Their homeland, then in ruins, provides very little evidence of personal

---

[436] Stern, 25.

[437] Miller and Hayes, 433.

[438] Miller and Hayes, 433.

presence and activity over the fifty years or so of exile.

In contrast to other studies, this work finds the Egyptian Gola a possible audience for Deutero-Isaiah, and incorporates the most recent archaeological data to support the Chroniclers' account which reports that there basically was no resident audience in the city of Jerusalem. The lack of an audience of survivors may then possibly imply that the texts, where Zion/Jerusalem are directly addressed, refer to those in exile, or the land itself from the perspective of future inhabitants.

The second focus of this research was the intended audiences. The opinions of seven prominent commentators and three additional authorities on the context of Deutero-Isaiah, were reviewed. The outcome of this study reveals that there are two basic schools of thought--those who argue that Deutero-Isaiah addressed an audience in Jerusalem as well as in Babylonia; and those who argue that the Babylonian exiles are the primary audience and those left in Jerusalem are insignificant. Both schools of thought recognize some minor presence in Judah. The first school of thought includes Westermann and Whybray who argue that Deutero-Isaiah has the whole nation in mind when he speaks. The second school of thought includes Brueggemann, Hanson and Clifford, who have concluded that the language of Isa 40-55 centers on exiles in need of release and return. The examination of the texts and the several scholars reveal at least the literary presence of additional audiences: Cyrus, sub-groups of the Babylonian exiles, the nations, and finally the land itself. What proves to be difficult is identifying these audiences with the groups formally named in the texts: Jacob/Israel; Zion/Jerusalem; Zion/Israel, Zion and Israel alone. There is some consensus around the identity of the groups, but even within the consensus there are double meanings that contribute to the confusion (e.g. Zion as both the city and the exiles). However, the textual and archaeological evidence seems to favor the exilic community as the primary audience.

It is the conclusion of chapter two that the primary audience is the Babylonian exiles with minor audiences addressed as a strategy to encourage the exiles to move from a place of captivity to a place of restoration and true comfort. This destination place is Zion, or the city of Jerusalem.

The third and final focus of this research involves defining the full agenda of comfort for Deutero-Isaiah. The agenda is multi-faceted. It includes: forgiveness of past sins; release from present exile; return to Jerusalem because it is the only place where God's presence truly dwells and the only place from which the message of salvation can fully go forth. It involves the installation of Israel as "Yahweh's Servant." Those in exile who are to return are called to a task. This task of the Servant involves many roles traditionally assigned to the king, as well as returning to Jerusalem and accepting the role as witness to all the nations. This witness now invites all peoples to respond to the message of comfort.

What makes this research different from other studies is the importance placed on the identity of the audiences and the direct connection between the audience and the components of the message of comfort. Prior studies do not give adequate attention to the identity of the audience and often fail to connect the audience with the message. Some of the works reviewed in this research even avoid making a commitment as to the identity of the audience. The result is that their positions are vague and leave the reader to reach his or her own conclusions, unaided.

The approach offered here has relied heavily on biblical, extra-biblical, and recent archaeological data as resources to unlock the mystery of the audience and message of Deutero-Isaiah. The compilation of this information helps create another perspective on what is at stake for Deutero-Isaiah in commissioning the servant and in stressing the vital importance of a return to Zion/Jerusalem.

The historical-critical method used by the commentators and other authorities on Isa 40-55, have, in combination, provided valuable information that led to insights that were not necessarily visible in separate interpretations of Deutero-Isaiah. For example, Clifford, Hanson and Whybray highlight God's role as husband in the text. This metaphor for God reminds the audience of the intimate connection that still exists between God and Israel. These, and other combined collected insights, offer a new lens of analysis by which the audiences and message of Deutero-Isaiah are more clearly defined. The people are comforted and encouraged. They are given a task, and Zion/Jerusalem is to become the true center whose message of the redeeming God will attract not only the scattered exiles but the distant nations as well.

BIBLIOGRAPHY

Abma, Richtsge. "Traveling from Babylon to Zion: Location and its Function in Isaiah 49-55." In Journal for the Study of the Old Testament 74 (1997): 3-28.

Ackroyd, Peter. Exile and Restoration. Philadelphia: Westminster, 1968.

Aharoni, Yohanan. The MacMillan Bible Atlas, ed. Yohanan Aharoni and Michael Avi- 3rd edition, Anson F. Rainey, Ze'ev Safrai. New York: Macmillan, 1993.

Albertz, Rainer. A History of Israelite Religion in the Old Testament Period Vol. II: From the Exile to the Maccabees. Louisville: Westminster John Knox Press, 1992.

Albright, W. F. Archaeology of Palestine. London: Pelican, 1956.

Anderson, Bernhard W. "Exodus Typology in Second-Isaiah." In Israel's Prophetic Heritage: Essays in Honor of James Muilenburg, ed. Bernhard Anderson and Walter Harrelson, 177-195. New York: Harper and Row, 1962.

Baltzer, Klaus. Deutero-Isaiah. Minneapolis: Fortress Press, 2001.

_____. "Liberation from Debt Slavery After the Exile in Second Isaiah and Nehemiah." In Ancient Israelite Religion, ed. Patrick D. Miller, Paul D. Hanson, and S. Dean McBride, 477-484. Philadelphia: Fortress Press, 1987.

_____. "The Polemic Against the Gods and its Relevance for Second Isaiah's Conception of the New Jerusalem." In Second Temple Studies, 2, Temple Community in the Persian Period, ed. Tamara C. Eskenazi and Kent Richards. Sheffield: JSOT Press, 1994: 52-59.

Barkay, G. "Iron Age II-III." In The Archaeology of Ancient Israel. New Haven: The Open University of Israel, 1992.

Berquist, Jon L. Judaism in Persian's Shadow: A Social and Historical Approach. Minneapolis: Fortress Press, 1995.

Bickerman, E.J. "Captivity." In The Cambridge History of Judaism. Vol. 1, ed. W.D. Davies and I. Findelstein. 1984: 324-358. Quoted in Rainer

Albertz, A History of Israelite Religion in the Old Testament Period Vol.II: From the Exile to the Maccabees, 599, n.21-22. Louisville: Westminster John Knox Press, 1992.

Bright, John. A History of Israel. Philadelphia: Westminster Press, 1972.

Brueggemann, Walter. "At the Mercy of Babylon: A Subversive Rereading of the Empire." A Social Reading of the Old Testament, ed. Patrick D. Miller, 111-132. Minneapolis: Fortress Press, 1994.

_____. A Commentary on Jeremiah: Exile and Homecoming. Grand Rapids: Eerdmans, 1998.

_____. Hopeful Imagination: Prophetic Voices in Exile. Philadelphia: Fortress Press, 1986.

_____. Isaiah 40-66. Louisville: Westminster John Knox Press, 1998.

_____. The Land. Philadelphia: Fortress Press, 1977.

_____. Old Testament Theology. Minneapolis: Fortress Press, 1992.

Carroll, Robert P. "The Myth of the Empty Land." In Semeia 59 (1992): 79-93.

Carter, Charles E. The Emergence of Yehud in the Persian Period: A Social and Demographic Study. Sheffield: Sheffield Academic, 1999.

Childs, Brevard. Isaiah. Louisville: Westminster John Knox Press, 2001.

Clements, R.E. Jeremiah. Atlanta: John Knox Press, 1988.

_____. "Zion as Symbol and Political Reality: A Central Isaianic Quest." In Studies in the Book of Isaiah, ed. J. Van Ruiten and M. Vervenne, 3-17. Leuven: Leuven University Press, 1997.

Clifford, Richard J. Fair Spoken and Persuading: An Interpretation of Second Isaiah. New York: Paulist Press, 1984.

Cogan, Mordechai. "Intro Exile: From the Assyrian Conquest to the Fall of Babylon." In The Oxford History of the Biblical World, ed. Michael D. Coogan, 242-275. New York: Oxford University Press, 1998.

_____ and Hayim Tadmor. II Kings. The Anchor Bible.Vol.11. New York: Doubleday, 1988.

Coogan, Michael D. West Semitic Names in the Mur_sâ Documents. Missoula: Scholars Press, 1976.

Cornfield, Gaalyah and Noel Freedman. Archaeology of the Bible, Book by Book. San Francisco: Harper and Row, 1976.

Dandameyev, Muhammed A. "A Social Stratification in Babylonia (7th-4th centuries B.C.E.)." Acta Antiqua 22 (1974): 433-44.

Fabry, Heinz-Josef. "___." In Theological Dictionary of the Old Testament, Vol. 5, ed. G.J.Botterweck et all. Translated by David E. Green, 366-384 Grand Rapids: Eerdmans, 1998.

Franke, Chris. Isaiah 46, 47, 48: A New Literary-Critical Reading. Winona Lake: Eisenbrauns, 1994.

Goldingay, John. "What Happens to Ms. Babylon in Isaiah 47, Why, and Who Says So?" In Tyndale Bulletin 47 (1996): 215-243.

Gottwald, Norman K. "Social Class and Ideology in Isaiah 40-55: An Eagletonian Reading." In Ideological Criticism in Biblical Texts, ed. D. Jobling and T. Pippin. Semeia 59 (1992): 43-57.

Hanson, Paul D. The Dawn of the Apocalyptic. Philadelphia: Fortress Press, 1979.

_____. Isaiah 40-66. Louisville: John Knox Press, 1995.

_____. "Israelite Religion in the Early Postexilic Period." In Ancient Israelite Religion, ed. Patrick D. Miller, Jr., Paul D. Hanson, and S. Dean McBride, 485-508. Philadelphia: Fortress Press, 1987.

Hermission, Hans-Jürgen. "Die Frau Zion." In Studies in the Book of Isaiah, ed. J. Van Ruiten and M. Vervenne, 19-39. Leuven: Leuven University Press, 1997.

Hoerth, Alfred J. Archaeology and the Old Testament. Grand Rapids: Baker Books, 1998.

Hyatt, James Philip. "Jeremiah." In Interpreters Bible, Vol. 5, ed. George A.

Buttrick et al.,777-1142. New York: Abingdon Press, 1956.

Jones, Douglass. "Cessation of Sacrifice After 586 B.C.E." In Journal of Theological Studies, N.S., Vol. XIV, Part 1, (April, 1963):13-31.

Jones, Richard N. and Zbigniew T. Fiema. "Tahpanhes." In Anchor Bible Dictionary. Vol. 5, 308-309. New York: Doubleday, 1992.

Josephus, Flavius. The Jewish Antiquities Book X. 6. Translated by H. St. J. Thackeray et al. Loeb Classical Library. Cambridge: Harvard University Press, 1926-1965.

Kaufman, Yehezkel. The Babylonian Captivity. Vol. IV, Ch 1,2. In History of the Religion of Israel. New York: Union of American Hebrew Congregations, 1970

Kenyon, Kathleen M. Digging Up Jerusalem. New York: Praeger Publishers, 1974.

Klein, Ralph W. Israel in Exile: A Theological Interpretation. Philadelphia: Fortress Press, 1979.

Knight, George A.F. Isaiah 40-55: Servant Theology. Grand Rapids: Eerdmanns, 1984.

Levenson, Jon D. Sinai and Zion. San Francisco: Harper and Row, 1985.

Mazar, Amihai. Archaeology of the Land of the Bible. New York: Doubleday, 1990.

McKenzie, John. Second Isaiah. Vol. 20. New York: The Anchor Bible Doubleday, 1968.

Melugin, Roy F. The Formation of Isaiah 40-55. New York: Walter de Gruyter, 1976.

_____. "Isaiah and the Nations in Isaiah 40-55." Problems in Biblical Theology Essays in Honor of Rolf Knierim, ed. Henry T.C. Sun and Keith L. Eades with James M. Robinson and Garth I. Moller, 249-264. Grand Rapids: Eerdmans, 1997.

Merendino, Rosario Pius. Der Erste und Der Letzte: Eine Untersuchung von Jes 40-48. Supplements to Vetus Testamentum, ed. J.A. Emerton et al.

Vol. XXXI. Leiden: E.J. Brill, 1981.

Miller, J. Maxwell and John Hayes. A History of Ancient Israel and Judah. Philadelphia: Westminster, 1986.

Miller, Patrick D., Paul D. Hanson, and S. Dean McBride. Ancient Israelite Religion. Philadelphia: Fortress Press, 1987.

Muilenburg, James. "Second Isaiah." Interpreters Bible. Vol. 5. ed. George A. Buttrick et al., 422-652. New York: Abingdon Press, 1962.

O'Connor, Kathleen M. "Speak Tenderly to Jerusalem: Second Isaiah's Reception and Use of Daughter Zion." In The Princeton Seminary Bulletin. Vol. XX, no. 3, n.s. (1999): 281-294.

Oded, Bustenay. "Judah and the Exile." In Israelite and Judean History, ed. J. M. Miller and J.H. Hayes, 435-488. Philadelphia: Westminster, 1986.

Ollenburger, Ben C. Zion the City of the Great King. Sheffield: JSOT Press, 1987.

Orlinsky, Harry M. "A Light of Nations"- "A Covenant of People." In Studies on the Second Part of the Book of Isaiah. Supplements to Vetus Testamentum, ed. G.W. Anderson et al., Vol. XIV, 97-117. Leiden: Brill, 1967.

Naidoff, Bruce D. "The Rhetoric of Encouragement in Isaiah 40:12-31: A Form-Critical Study." In VT 31 (1981), 63-77.

Parunak, H. Van dyke. "A Semantic Survey of NHM." In Biblical 56, (1975):500-530.

Pritchard, James B. Ancient Near Eastern Texts Relating to the Old Testament. Princeton: Princeton University Press, 1969.

Roberts, J.J.M. "Isaiah in Old Testament Theology." In Interpreting the Prophets, ed. James Luther Mays and Paul J. Achtemeir. Philadelphia: Fortress Press, 1987.

Seitz, Christopher. Zion's Final Destiny. Minneapolis: Fortress Press, 1991.

Simon, U.E. A Theology of Salvation: A Commentary on Isaiah 40-55. London: SPCK, 1953.

Smith, Daniel. Religion of the Landles: The Social Context of the Babylonian Exile. Bloomington: Meyer Stone Books, 1989.

Smith-Christopher, Daniel. "Reassessing the Historical and Sociological Impact of the Babylon Exile 597/587-539 B.C.E." In Exile: Old Testament, Jewish, and Christian Conceptions, ed. James M. Scott, 7-36. Supplements to the Journal for the Study of Judaism, Vol. 56. New York: Brill, 1997.

Snaith, Norman H. "Isaiah 40-66: A Study of the Teaching of the Second Isaiah and its Consequences." In Studies on the Second Part of the Book of Isaiah. Supplements to Vetus Testamentum, Vol. XIV, ed. G.W. Anderson et al., 139-165. Leiden: E.J. Brill, 1967.

Steinmann, Jean. Le Livre de la Consolation d'Israel et les Prophètes du Retour de l'Exil. (The Book of the Consolation of Israel and the Prophets of the return from Exile). Paris: Les Editions Du Cerf, 1960.

Stern, Ephraim. In Archaeology of the Land of the Bible. New York: Doubleday, 2001.

Stoebe, H.J. "___." In Theologisches Handworteerauch zum Alten Testament, ed. Ernst Jenni and Claus Westermann. Zurich: Kaiser Verlag Munchen Theologischer Verlag, 1976.

Thompson, Henry O. "Chebar." In Anchor Bible Dictionary, ed. David Noel Freeman. New York: Doubleday, 1992

Torey, C.C. "The Exile and the Restoration," in Ezra Studies. New York: Ktav, 1910, 1970. 285-340.

Watts, John D. W. Isaiah 34-66. Word Bible Commentary. Vol. 25. Waco: Word Book, 1987.

Weinburg, S.S. "Post-Exilic Palestine: An Archaeological Report." In Proceedings of the Israel Academy of Science and Humanities. 4 (1971):

Weinfeld, M. Social Justice in Ancient Israel and in the Ancient Near East. Philadelphia: Fortress Press, 1995.

Weissbach, F.H. Das Hauptheiligtum des Marduk in Babylon. Leipzig: Hinrichs, 1938.

Wellard, James. By the Waters of Babylon. London: Hutchinson and Company, 1972.

Westermann, Claus. Isaiah 40-66. Philadelphia: Westminster Press, 1969.

Whitley, Charles Francis. The Exilic Age. London: Longmans, Green and Company: 1957.

Whybray, R.N. Isaiah 40-66. Grand Rapids: Eerdmans, 1975.

Wiseman, Donald John. Chronicles of the Chaldean Kings. London: The Trustees of the British Museum, 1956.

_____. Nebuchadrezzar and Babylon. Oxford: Oxford University Press, 1984.

Wilson, Robert R. "The Community of Second Isaiah." In Reading and Preaching the Book of Isaiah, ed. C.R. Seitz. Minneapolis: Fortress Press, 1988: 53-70.

Yamauchi, Edwin M. Persia and the Bible. Grand Rapids: Baker Books, 1990.

GENERAL INDEX

Abraham, Sarah, 79,85,91,126,128,143,149
Albright, 17
archaeology, 2,12,15,18,20,23,24,25,29,33, 37,39,56,159,160,161,162,164,165,166
audience, 1,2,3,39,41,42,43,44,45,46,47,48, 49,51,53,54,55,56,57,58,59,60,62,63,64, 65,66,67,68,69,70,72,74,75,76,77,78,79, 80,81,82,84,89,92,93,96,98,99,101,102, 105,107,108,109,110,114,115,116,118, 126, 127,128,131,133,135,143,149,159, 164,165,166
Babylon, 1,2,3,4,5,6,8,9,10,11,12,13,14,15, 16,17,18,19,20,21,24,25,26,27,28,29,32, 33,34,35,39,40,45,46,49,51,55,56,58,62, 63,64,65,66,67,68,68,70,71,72,734,75,76, 81,83,84,85,87,89,91,94,96,98,100,104, 106,107,108,110,111,112,113,114,115,117, 121,123,125,133,134,135,136,137,138,139, 140,141,142,143,146,147,148,149,151,160, 161,162,163,164,165
Benjamin, 16,19,20,21,23,24,35,39,77,102,160
Berquist, 20,25,161
Bride of Yahweh, 57,58,96
Chaldeans, 6,7,8,9,17,19
comfort, 1,2,3,45,50,54,56,72,74,77,87,88, 104,114,115,116,117,118,119,120,121,122, 123,125,127,128,129,130,131,133,134,137, 140,143,149,150,154,155,156,157,159,165,166
covenant, 61,86,137,152,153
creation, 53,70,84,123,129,149,155,157
2 Chronicles, 7,10,16,108,159,160,161
Chronicles of Chaldeans Kings, 9,10,11,13,14
Cyrus, 1,46,49,53,62,70,71,87,89,100,108,113, 118,122,145,148,158,164
David, 91,100,108,137,143,148,149,153,158
deportation, 2,7,9,14,16,17,18,22,23,26,33,39, 47,51,65,103,104
Diaspora, 2,28,36,90,93,97,98,126,130,144,157
Divine Council, 149
Eagletonian Ideology, 105,106,107,109
Eden, 125
Egypt, 5,7,8,10,17,22,35,36,37,39,42,98,102, 138,151,153,160,163

exilic/exilic period, 2,8,9,23,26,28, 29,30,31,32,33,34,35,38,39,41, 42,43,44,46,47,48,49,50,51,52, 53,54,55,56,57,58,59,60,61,62, 63,64,66,67,68,69,71,72,74,75, 76,77,78,79,80,82,83,84,85,86, 87,88,89,90,91,94,109,110,111
Exodus, 64,72,125,136,138,140,141, 142,149,150,157
Ezekiel, 11,21,23,26,27,31,32,33,94, 108,111,145,154,162,163
forgiveness, 121,122,123,126,140, 149,157,161,165
Gedaliah, 6,7,16,17,19,22,35,160, 163
go'el/gola, 92,149
Ishmael, 6,19,22,25
Israel, 42,54,57,60,61,63,68,69,70, 71,72,79,80,81,82,85,86,87,99, 100,102,104,105,107,109,110, 112,113,114,116,117,118,120, 121,122,123,124,125,127,135, 136,137,139,140,141,142,143, 147,148,149,150,151,152,153, 154,155,157,158,156,166
Jacob/Israel, 1,44,46,52,53,54,60, 61,67,68,79,84,85,86,92,93, 94,96,98,109,114,164
Jehoikim, 4,5,7,10,11
Jehoikin, 4,5,7,9,11,27,34,162
Jeremiah, 7,8,10,16,19,21,22,23,26, 32,33,35,37,108,113,159,160, 162,163
Jerusalem, 1,5,6,7,8,9,10,11,12,13, 14,17,18,20,21,23,24,25,26,31, 38,39,41,44,45,46,50,54,55,57 58,59,60,64,65,72,77,78,79,83, 84,67,88,90,91,92,93,94,95,96, 97,98,100,101,104,105,107, 108,109,110,114,115,116,119, 121,123,125,127,128,129,130, 131,132,133,138,140,143,144, 145,146,147,148,149,150,157,

158,160,161,163,164,165
Jones, Douglass, 22
Josephus, 10,161
Judah, 1,2,4,6,7,9,10,12,14,16,17,18,20,
    21,24,25,26,35,37,41,42,44,45,46,53,
    54,56,57,58,59,65,66,69,74,81,83,84,
    85,91,93,97,101,104,105,106,110,111,
    114,116,127,134,135,145,146,160,161,
    163,164
Kenyon, Kathleen, 13,25,161
2 Kings, 7,16,19,21,35,108,136,159,161
Lachish, 12,13
Lamentations, 17,18,131
Land, 1,29,39,46,51,64,65,68,69,70,75,
    77,79,80,83,84,85,88,89,94,100,101,
    102,103,104,105,106,108,109,110,
    111,113,114,122,125,126,127,137,139,
    143,144,145,160,161,163,164,
Mizpah, 6,7,16,17,19,24,25,160,163
Moses, 125,136,137,141
myth of the empty land, 102,104
nations, 2,41,42,43,44,45,46,50,51,53,54,
    63,65,66,68,69,70,72,75,76,80,81,83,
    88,89,97,98,107,109,114,117,118,123,
    124,127,129,130,147,148,150,151,152,
    153,154,155,156,157,163,164,165,166
nhm, 3,118,119,120,121,157
Nebuchadrezzar, 4,5,6,7,8,9,10,11,19,26,
    30,35,37,39,56,112,136,160
Noah, 91,137,143,149
Palestine, 15,136,150
poorest in the land, 5,6,13,16,19,20,56,
    103,160
remnant, 8,35,44,56,67,68,94
Sabbath, 8,16,32,39,103,161
Servant, 2,3,41,42,46,49,60,61,62,63,71,
    72,79,80,81,89,90,91,94,95,98,100,101,
    109,117,122,125,127,135,139,140,141,
    142,146,149,150,151,152,153,154,155,
    156,157,165,166
Servant Song, 122,152,156
Stern, E., 14,15,17,20,25,102,160,161,162
Temple, 23,31,32,36,37,38,39,60,70,71,103
vineyard(s), 8
waste places, 130,157
Wiseman, Donald, 9,10,11

witness(es), 48,54,69,70,79,81,98,
    130,143,153,154,157,165
worship, 2,32
Zedekiah, 5,7,8,11,19,27
Zion, 22,27,51,58,59,63,64,65,66,
    67,68,71,72,78,79,86,87,88,95,
    96,97,101,117,119,120,121,122,
    123,124,125,126,127,128,130,
    131,132,133,134,135,136,137,
    138,141,142,144,146,147,148,
    149,150,153,154,156,157,165
Zion/Jerusalem, 1,40,41,44,46,50,54,
    57,58,77,78,79,86,92,93,95,96,
    97,98,114,116,117,119,125,
    126,130,133,143,144,145,146,
    149,155,157,164,166

www.ingramcontent.com/pod-product-compliance
Lightning Source LLC
Chambersburg PA
CBHW052051300426
44117CB00012B/2071